Lieutenant William Collins King, Burma, 1945.

DEDICATED TO MY FAMILY

Insignia Key

The Castle
The official insignia of the U.S. Army Corps of Engineers

The Shield
The official insignia of the China-Burma-India Theater. The background for the stars is royal blue; the vertical stripes are red and white.

The single campaign bar
Medal for the Asiatic-Pacific Campaign (Pages 21, 35, 71, 89, 95, 111, and 151) It contains bronze stars for participation relative to combat in the India-Burma Campaign and the Central Burma Campaign.

> Colors: Yellow background, two white side bands with red stripes in the middle, and a center band with dark blue, white, and red stripes.

The triple campaign bar
Includes medals (left to right) for:

The American Campaign (Pages 1, 5, and 13)

> Colors: Royal blue background, two white side bands with dark blue and red stripes, and a narrow middle band with dark blue, white, and red stripes.

The World War II Victory Medal (Page 193)

> Colors: Wide red middle band with narrow yellow stripes on either side; two royal blue side bands with a narrower yellow band having a middle red stripe.

The Army of Occupation (Pages 167 & 175)

> Colors: Two narrow white side bands; a left of middle black band, and a right of middle red band.

BUILDING *for* VICTORY

WORLD WAR II IN CHINA, BURMA, AND INDIA
and the 1875th Engineer Aviation Battalion

William Collins King

TAYLOR TRADE PUBLISHING
Lanham • New York • Dallas • Boulder • Toronto • Oxford

Published by Taylor Trade Publishing
An imprint of The Rowman & Littlefield Publishing Group, Inc.
4501 Forbes Boulevard, Suite 200
Lanham, Maryland 20706

Distributed by National Book Network

William Collins King, Author
Louise King Sturgess, Editor
Diane Tarquinio Goodwin and Beth Buckholtz, Designers

Copies of these memoirs and the personal records and papers of the writer have been donated to:
Library & Archives
Senator John Heinz Pittsburgh Regional History Center
1212 Smallman Street, Pittsburgh, PA 15222
Phone: 412-454-6364 Fax: 412-454-6028 E-mail: library@hswp.org
Website: www.pghhistory.org

 Historical Society
of Western Pennsylvania

The Senator John Heinz Pittsburgh Regional History Center is owned and operated
by the Historical Society of Western Pennsylvania.

Library of Congress Cataloging-in-Publication Data

King, William C., 1921–
    Building for victory : World War II in China, Burma, and India and the 1875th
    Engineer Aviation Battalion / William C. King.—1st Taylor Trade Publishing ed.
        p. cm.
    Includes bibliographical references.
    ISBN 1-58979-099-5 (alk. paper)
    1. King, William C. 2. United States. Army. Engineer Aviation Battalion, 1875th.
    3. United States. Army—Officers—Biography. 4. World War, 1939–1945—Personal
    narratives, American. 5. World War, 1939–1945—Regimental histories—United
    States. 6. World War, 1939–1945—Campaigns—China. 7. World War, 1939–1945—
    Campaigns—Burma. 8. World War, 1939–1945—Campaigns—India. I. Title.

    D769.3351875th .K56 2004
    940.54'4973'092—dc22   2004041241
    [B]

Acknowledgments

This book is dedicated to my family, all of whom were concerned about my safe return from military service. I have been fortunate to be part of a close and loving family. In 1943 my family included:

- my mother and father, sister, and maternal grandmother Charlotte Y. Collins;

- my father's sister, Aunt Ruth, who was a professional artist, petite but indomitable, gracious, and with a lively sense of humor;

- my mother's brother, Uncle Morris, who served as a Lieutenant Commander in the Navy, and his son Morrie. I had a chance but special meeting with Uncle Morris in Oran, North Africa; and

- two paternal grandparents: Grandfather William King and Grandmother Gertrude Raffington King.

For my parents, my entering the military must have been especially trying, since we, as much of the nation, had had a difficult time during the Great Depression.

As I write this memoir in 2002–2003, my family has grown to include Carol (née Thorne), my wife of 51 years, and our three sons and daughters-in-law, one daughter and son-in-law, and 13 grandchildren, plus numerous relatives, who are in close touch with one another.

Fortunately we have not experienced parental concerns about anyone in our family serving in the military forces. The most poignant expression we have read of this parental concern is an inscription engraved on the headstone of a young British officer who died at the Battle of El Alamein in Egypt in 1942. It reads:

"To all the World he was only one.
To us he was all the World."

Many have contributed to this book, including all my companions in the 1875th Engineer Aviation Battalion, those responsible for the sources listed at the end of the introduction and in the bibliography, and numerous individuals mentioned and not mentioned, who were vital in determining or reporting what happened.

Special acknowledgments are accorded to the following, who played key roles in the creation of the book itself:

- C. Hax McCullough: a close friend, who has a sparkling wit and is a superb mentor. Hax founded a successful publishing company, McCullough Communications, and spent his career in public relations and promoting interest in Pittsburgh history. I thank him for setting such high standards for this book.

- Lieutenant John A. Power: a fellow officer in the 1875th Engineer Aviation Battalion, its Adjutant in the latter stages of the war, my companion on the leave in Kashmir, and the author of the battalion's history.

- The U.S. Army Signal Corps, which provided photographs, including those of Colonel Seagrave, the Salween River bridge and gorge, and the initial convoy from Ledo to Kunming, among others.

- David S. Ketchum: a close friend; an avid student of World War II history; a recipient of the Soldier's Medal, the Bronze Star, and the Commendation Medal; and a participant in nine campaigns in the European-African-Middle Eastern Theater of Operations. Dave provided the two books, *The Ciano Diaries, 1939–1943* and *Mussolini*.

- Sergeant David B. Richardson: a World War II correspondent for *YANK*, the global U.S. Army weekly magazine. His most notable assignment was to accompany the famed Merrill's Marauders on their campaign behind Japanese lines in Burma. He also accompanied Australian infantry in jungle fighting in New Guinea, B-24 bombers and PT boats in the Battle of the Bismarck Sea, B-25 "Bridgebuster" bombers in Burma, and Gurkha paratroops in the capture of Rangoon. Following the war he served as a foreign correspondent on five continents, first with *Time* and *Life* magazines, and later with *U.S. News & World Report*. Dave authored the summary of the Burma Campaign on pages 105–107.

- Edward Gariepy, whose father was a fine soldier in Company A, and whom I remember well. Ed provided the roster for the entire battalion, included in the appendix of this book, and several pictures.

- William H. Reed, Jr.: the copilot of the B-29, *Deacon's Disciples II*. He provided the information about his crew's experience in their 20 combat missions against the Japanese, and related pictures.

- Grant Gerlich, curator of the Soldiers & Sailors National Military Museum & Memorial, for allowing us to photograph the World War II medals for use as chapter headings.

- Diane Tarquinio Goodwin and Beth Buckholtz: designers of the book, and Shelli Mullen and Karena Apicella, for photographic services.

- Louise King Sturgess: my daughter, and editor of this book. In her role as Executive Director of the Pittsburgh History & Landmarks Foundation, she has edited many books on the region's architecture.

- Carol Thorne King: my dear wife, who has always been my strongest supporter and inspiration. She was remarkably patient and understanding during the months I spent researching, writing, and editing this manuscript.

My parents and I corresponded throughout the war. My father had every letter he received from me retyped and bound in a booklet. Notice the stamps and postal marks on the envelopes.

The joining of the Ledo and Burma Roads: February 1945. Courtesy of U.S. Army Signal Corps.

Contents

Maps

Maps drawn by the author.

Father and son in 1943, at 208 Gladstone Road, Pittsburgh, Pa.:
William Raffington and Lieutenant William Collins King.

Introduction

This book recounts my military experiences leading to and during World War II. There was nothing heroic about my war service. Although I was in combat zones, and on one occasion could hear heavy artillery fire, I was never exposed to combat. But my military service did represent a unique and remarkable experience, certainly one I never would have had otherwise.

I was born in Pittsburgh, Pennsylvania, and grew up there in an attractive residential neighborhood known as Squirrel Hill. My parents had come from Chicago. My one sibling, Barbara, was two years older than I. In July of 1943 she applied for admission to the Officer Candidate School of the U.S. Marine Corps Women's Reserve. On September 22 she enrolled in the Officer Candidate School at Camp Lejeune, North Carolina. On November 15 she graduated and was sworn in as a Second Lieutenant in the Marine Corps Reserve. She was immediately assigned as Company Commander, Company B, Women's Reserve Battalion, Quantico, Virginia. The officers of this company taught many of the courses held for male Marines at Quantico. The enlisted women filled many of the service functions needed in operating that base. She held this position until her discharge on June 12, 1945, as a First Lieutenant.

My father graduated from high school in Chicago and went into business. In the early 1900s he joined a small machine-tool sales agency

Daughter and mother in 1943, at 208 Gladstone Road, Pittsburgh, Pa.: Barbara Jean King, USMC, and Anne Collins King.

in Pittsburgh and became sales manager. My mother graduated from Northwestern University and was awarded membership in the Phi Beta Kappa scholastic honors society. My parents enjoyed a close and harmonious marriage. Never did my sister or I hear an angry word between them, nor a single word of off-color language. Their integrity was close to absolute and they expected the same from us. They trusted us without reservation; and we could not imagine doing anything to betray that trust. They had an infectious zest for life and a sparkling sense of humor. It was a fun family.

My war experience involved a remarkable journey to fascinating cultures worlds apart from the one in which I grew up. It was a journey that would encompass three and one-half years and circumnavigation of the globe.

My overseas service was primarily in India and Burma,[1] a remote and little understood theater of the war. The American involvement there was of comparable duration to that in Europe and the Pacific. The fighting was intense and the conditions grueling. In the Kohima-Imphal battle there were approximately 150,000 combatants on the two sides. The Japanese soldiers were superbly trained and led, and often fought to the death. The Allied forces included Chinese and American troops moving south along the Ledo Road through northern and central Burma, Chinese troops moving west along the Burma Road from the Salween River into central Burma, and Indian and British troops moving south from India through west-central Burma. Each side was at the extreme end of their nation's supply line, so lack of replacements, exhaustion, and starvation were ever present. The climate was tropical, with disease and the monsoon rains taking an awful toll on both armies. The terrain where much of the fighting occurred was covered with dense forests, and included many large rivers and massive mountain ranges. Trails and roads had to be cut for hundreds of miles. Much of the travel by the combatants and their supporting units was on foot, with supplies carried on their backs, by mules, or dropped from airplanes.

The 1875th Engineer Aviation Battalion was a service organization. We built airfields in western Bengal from which the U.S. Air Force's

[1]Following World War II, Burma obtained its independence from Great Britain and changed its name to Myanmar. The name Burma is used throughout this book.

B-29 bombers first attacked Japan. We then participated in building the Ledo Road, the principal supply artery for the combat troops in the north and central Burma Campaigns. After the Japanese were driven out of that area, the road became the principal route for supplying the Allied forces in China. The Allies in China had a twofold mission: first, to keep the large number of Japanese forces there from returning to their homeland to help defend against the planned Allied invasion, and second, to provide airbases closer to Japan to support the invasion.

My military service compressed into a mere 41 months challenges, successes, and failures that normally would have taken decades to experience. As a result, I left the service in May 1946 far more mature and self-assured than otherwise would have been possible.

My military experience initiated a sequence of events that led to a very fulfilling life, including meeting my wonderful wife, caring for our family, pursuing a successful career with Gulf Oil Corporation, and serving on the boards of trustees of several nonprofit organizations. As chairman of the board of trustees of the Historical Society of Western Pennsylvania from 1986 to 1997 I helped lead the effort to establish the Senator John Heinz Pittsburgh Regional History Center.

* * *

This book has been written to document a remarkable period in my life for my family, friends, and any who served in the China-Burma-India Theater (CBI) during World War II. Too little is known about the dramatic events that transpired there. Perhaps this book and other firsthand accounts will encourage a broader interest and understanding.

In writing this book, I have utilized my official personal military record, my battalion's official history, the collection of my frequent letters home (which my father had typed soon after they arrived), my sister's war memoirs which include some references to my service, my collection of books about the war in the CBI, and my memory, which at 82 years of age is still impressive and reliable, according to my daughter. Picture captions include attribution, except for those taken by or for me.

William Collins King's dog tags; officer's "U.S." collar pin; captain's insignia (awarded on return to the U.S.); and the eagle insignia worn on the front of an officer's visored dress hat.

WORLD WAR II SYNOPSIS:
1939 – 41

The Nazi Germany imprisonment and extermination of Jews, the Holocaust, began in the 1930s and continued until the end of the war.

1939
August 23: Germany and the U.S.S.R. sign a mutual nonaggression pact.
September 1: Germany invades Poland, the U.S.S.R. follows.
September 3: Great Britain and France declare war on Germany.
Late September: Poland is occupied by Germany and the U.S.S.R.

1940, January – June
The Battle of the Atlantic Ocean starts; German submarines sink Allied shipping.
April: Germany invades Denmark and Norway; both are quickly occupied.
May: Germany overruns Holland and Belgium.
  Germans surround 340,000 British troops in the Low Countries,
  but they are successfully evacuated to Britain.
  Germany invades France.
June: Italy declares war on Britain and France.
  France capitulates.

1940, July – December
Battle of the Atlantic continues.
July: The air battle over Britain starts.
  President F. D. Roosevelt cuts off exports to Japan of steel and other products.
August: Germany starts bombing British cities.
September: Italian forces in Libya attack Egypt.
December: British forces drive Italian forces back into Libya.

1941, January – June
Battle of the Atlantic: German submarines gaining upper hand.
President F. D. Roosevelt freezes Japanese funds in the U.S.
General Erwin Rommel takes command of Germany's Afrika Corps.
March: U.S. passes Lend-Lease Act, authorizing the nation to lend or lease
  strategic materials and equipment to its allies.
April: Germany occupies Yugoslavia and Greece.
May: Germany occupies the Island of Crete in the Mediterranean Sea.
  Germany withdraws from the air battle over Britain.
June 22: Germany invades the U.S.S.R.

1941, July – December
November: Germans surround Leningrad.
December: Germans reach Moscow; are driven back by U.S.S.R. counterattack.
  Japan bombs the U.S. fleet in Pearl Harbor, Hawaii.
  U.S., Canada, and Britain declare war on Japan.
  U.S. declares war on Germany and Italy; they retaliate.
  Thailand, Hong Kong, Guam, and Wake Island fall to the Japanese.
  The Japanese invade the Philippines and Burma.
  Germany achieves superiority in Battle of the Atlantic.

The Course of Events

This account begins in September 1939. On September 1 Hitler's Germany invaded Poland, precipitating World War II. That week I entered Carnegie Institute of Technology ("Carnegie Tech" and now Carnegie Mellon University) as a freshman, majoring in chemical engineering. It was only a five-minute walk to the campus from my parents' home on Gladstone Road in Pittsburgh. Our five academic courses were prescribed. In addition, each male freshman had to enroll in a four-year course, either in the Reserve Officer's Training Corps (ROTC) or physical training. Most of the sports lovers chose the latter, many of the nonathletes chose ROTC, as I did. The likelihood of the United States getting involved in World War II was high. Completing the ROTC course would assure my serving as an officer; choosing the physical training option would involve a high risk of being drafted as an enlisted man.

   In the fall of 1941 I started my junior year at Carnegie Tech. On Sunday, December 7, our family had a routine Sunday brunch at home and I then went up to my room to study. Shortly after noon my sister came up and asked me to come down to the living room and listen to the radio. I did — Pearl Harbor was unfolding before us. We sat in stunned silence. After we had heard what had happened I rose and returned to my studies. The prospects were too grave for petty talk. We knew I would be called into service and that it would be a long and dreadful war, both in Europe and Asia.

On the following day classes were recessed in midmorning. The entire college staff and student body gathered on the large lawn in front of the College of Fine Arts, where loudspeakers had been set up to broadcast President Roosevelt's address to Congress. This was his famous "a date which will live in infamy" speech. America declared war against Japan. It was a bright, warm, sunny day. I looked over the assembled group of fine young men and wondered how many would not survive the war. Three days later war was declared against Nazi Germany.

Life changed dramatically. Gasoline rationing limited personal use of automobiles. Travel by rail and bus was restricted. Some foods were rationed, such as sugar and butter. The nation geared up a massive effort for war production. Students became more serious in their work and some men chose to enlist in the service branch of their choice.

The following spring it became apparent to the school administration that pressure to draft college students was increasing rapidly. To enable our class to graduate before we might be drafted, the administration rescheduled the first semester of our senior year to the summer of 1942 and the second semester in the fall of 1942. In the summer only the senior engineering men and the senior women from Margaret Morrison College were involved. Without any extracurricular activities the frenetic collegiate pace moderated and we enjoyed a pleasant summer semester. However, it meant that the ROTC students could not attend the traditional and required ROTC summer camp. As a result, upon graduation we would have to complete the strenuous three-month Officer Candidate School (OCS).

In the fall, with military service only weeks away, my usually busy schedule of extracurricular activities was put aside to allow room for partying; as a result, my grades slipped, but not enough to affect graduation. At the start of the fall semester my best friend and fraternity brother, Nelson Crooks, talked me into joining him on the varsity soccer team. In mid-fall the ligaments in my right knee were badly strained during a game. The knee swelled and stiffened. I could not bend it and was not able to participate in ROTC drills and other physical activities. With intensive rehabilitation it improved considerably. At the end of the semester we had to pass a physical examination to qualify for admission to OCS. This included a deep-knee bend. I barely made a qualifying squat and, because of the pain, had to immediately stand erect. Fortunately the exam was rather perfunctory, and I passed.

On December 20 commencement exercises were held for the expedited seniors. The ROTC students received their diploma on the near side of the stage; then walked to the far side where they received their orders to report to OCS for their respective branch of service. Many of my classmates and I were ordered to report to the 26th OCS class at Fort Belvoir, Virginia.

During the holidays we spent treasured moments together as a family, and I had a number of dates with some of my friends from Carnegie Tech. At that time there was no way of knowing that it would be four years before I would have another Christmas at home.

WORLD WAR II SYNOPSIS:
1942-43

1942, January - June
U.S. and Britain assign top priority to the defeat of Germany, and then Japan.
Germany continues deadly assault on Allied shipping in the Atlantic.
January: Malaysia falls to the Japanese.
February: Singapore falls to the Japanese.
March: Netherlands East Indies falls to the Japanese; New Guinea is invaded.
April: Sixteen U.S. B-25 bombers, led by Lieutenant Colonel J. H. Doolittle and
  flying from aircraft carriers, bomb Japan.
  The Philippines fall to Japan.
May: The Japanese naval force is defeated in the Battle of the Coral Sea.
  Germany attacks the Caucasus in the U.S.S.R.
  Britain starts night saturation bombing of German cities.
June: At the Battle of Midway (Hawaiian chain of islands), the U.S. naval force
  decisively defeats the Japanese naval force.
  Japan occupies Guadalcanal Island in the Solomon Islands.

**The summer of 1942 marks the highpoint of the military campaigns of Germany and
Japan. From this date forward the Allied forces become increasingly successful.**

1942, July - December
The Battle of the Atlantic rages on.
The American Air Force starts the daylight pinpoint bombing of German cities.
July: Rommel's Afrika Corps advances into Egypt, and is stopped by the British.
August: The Germans reach the outskirts of Stalingrad.
  Rommel's Afrika Corps attacks the British at El Alamein and is repulsed.
  In the Pacific, the Battle of Guadalcanal starts.
October: The British counterattack at El Alamein, and start a rout of the Afrika Corps.
November: U.S.S.R. counterattacks at Stalingrad, starting a rout of the Germans there.
  American forces land in Algeria and Morocco, North Africa.
  U.S. forces attack the Japanese at Buna-Sanananda, New Guinea.

1943, January - June
January: In New Guinea, the Japanese are defeated in grueling battles in the Owen
  Stanley Mountains, and at Buna-Sanananda.
February: The German forces at Stalingrad surrender.
  The Japanese withdraw from the Guadalcanal.
May: The last Axis forces in North Africa surrender.
Midyear: Using convoys, long-range planes, and radar, the Allies are now sinking German
  submarines in the Atlantic faster than they can be made.

1943, July - December
July: Allies invade Sicily.
  Mussolini is ousted from the Italian government.
September: Italy surrenders, the Germans fight on fiercely in Italy.
  Allies invade southern Italy.
November: Tarawa Island in the Gilbert Islands is captured from the Japanese.

Survival of the Fittest

On January 7, 1943 my family drove me to the B&O Railroad Station in downtown Pittsburgh. We hugged good-bye. My dad gave me ten dollars, enough to last to the first pay day, and I boarded the train, together with many of my classmates. In midafternoon we arrived at Fort Belvoir, Virginia, on the Potomac River just south of Washington, D.C. In all there were 65 members of this OCS class, 28 from Penn State University and 37 from Carnegie Tech. We were divided into two sections, Company S and Company T.

All of us had followed previous instructions to travel light and bring only the barest of necessities. Our arrival precipitated consternation at the headquarters office. Since we had not completed our ROTC summer camp, we had not been sworn in as officers. In fact we had not been sworn into the armed forces at all. Military regulations prohibited issuing uniforms and military equipment to civilians. We spent the bitter cold week going through the prescribed training courses and field maneuvers in our civilian clothes and light outer garments, which were no match for the weather and our strenuous activities. By the end of the week the Army finally issued regulations permitting us to receive appropriate uniforms, clothing, rifles, and other necessary supplies. By then our civilian clothing was worn out, as were many of us. Our sedentary college life had ill equipped us for the rigors of winter training at Fort Belvoir. As a result, about 15 of my classmates came down with the flu,

Our OCS company officers. Lieutenant Palmer, second from left — the "very strict, but fair" officer.

Company S included 37 members. Three of us were fraternity brothers. First row, far right: Robert R. McCutcheon. Second row, third from right: William C. King. Top row, far left: John O. Chesley.

or pneumonia. This precluded them from completing the OCS course. They were returned to civilian life and most of them, being graduate engineers and in high demand, spent the war working in industry for the war production effort.

My section was supervised by a former regular army sergeant with many years of experience, Lieutenant Palmer. He had been commissioned an officer at the start of World War II and assigned to the Fort Belvoir OCS training staff. He had a thorough knowledge of the army, was very strict, but very fair. The candidates felt he was assigned to this job as an example of what an officer ought to be.

We quickly found that the staff was consistently strict and demanding, deliberately putting pressure on each candidate. They seemed to do this particularly in regard to insignificant matters. This was obviously a deliberate tactic to weed out candidates who lacked sufficient emotional control and physical stamina.

We lived in long, narrow, uninsulated, one-story plywood barracks. Each candidate had an iron cot with an overhead shelf, and a footlocker at the foot of the cot. Our belongings had to be precisely and immaculately arranged at all times. There were two pot-bellied, coal-burning stoves near each end of the barracks. They provided barely enough heat to keep water from freezing in the canteens. The common bathroom facilities were at the far end of the block from our building. Since we could only use them during free time, of which we had very little, they were always crowded. I managed to average about two showers a week during the entire time at Fort Belvoir.

Meals were rushed, and were of adequate quality, but sometimes skimpy in quantity. About ten of us were seated at each table in the mess hall and each week one of us was designated the server. The server was responsible for obtaining the food platters from the kitchen, and returning the dirty dishes and flatware. Our supervising officer continually emphasized that if there were any problems with the food they should be reported to him. One lunchtime when I was the server there was no food left on the serving platters when I sat down to eat after completing my deliveries. I felt that this was a very legitimate problem and reported it to the officer. He ordered me to stay in the mess hall after the other candidates returned to the barracks, and then provided me with a bowl piled full of strong, boiled cabbage and a plate full of cold Spam. He ordered me to eat all of it before returning to the barracks. I had to gobble all this down to avoid being late for the afternoon project, and almost got sick from eating so much distasteful food. That was the last time anyone in our class found any problems with the meals.

Mornings and afternoons were fully scheduled with either classroom sessions or rigorous field training. Field training comprised the bulk of the curriculum. Much of the classwork was new and important, but some was repetitious of our ROTC instruction at Carnegie Tech and the math was high school level. In such classes it was hard to keep alert. Jim Curry, a close friend, fraternity brother, and OCS classmate, wrote to our Carnegie Tech alumni magazine:

> We work hard all day and are in bed at 10:30. Then, after a few hours of backbreaking rest, we hear a whistle at 5:45. All during the day everyone gets a little sleepy. The prime example of sleeplessness personified is ignoble Willie King. Without fail he drops off the brink of consciousness every day, and when the instructors see him, oh, brothers! At first it was a reprimand, then he did three turns around a building at double time, and lastly, his crowning achievement was being beaned by a piece of chalk used as a projectile.

Such incidents undoubtedly contributed to my weekend restrictions.

Many of the field projects involved a "Hill 610." This must have been one of the most mapped, mined, fortified, defended, and assaulted sites in the entire war. We learned a lot about combat, weapons use and deployment, tactics, and survival. The projects were not overly challenging, but the weather was horrible. The temperature got as low as 10° Fahrenheit, the relative humidity was high, and the wind was vicious. We had standard GI winter clothing, but the knit wool gloves and GI helmets were little protection against the cold. At times our fingers got so stiff we could hardly hold our rifles.

Each class was required to take a 20-mile, overnight hike, carrying a full pack and rifle. There were a lot of Texans in our section. Shortly after we started hiking, they pulled out their plugs of chewing tobacco. Being gracious, they offered the rest of us a bite. I accepted. The first few chews were sweet and not unpleasant. Then suddenly my mouth caught fire, my head exploded, and I got horribly nauseated. I did not have the strength to continue hiking on my own and had to lean on the man ahead of me. That and the fact that it was a brisk, cold night saved me. After about an hour I recovered and was able to proceed on my own.

From about noon on Saturdays until Sunday evenings candidates had time off and could leave Fort Belvoir if they wished. However, if a candidate had not passed inspection, had been late for any function, or otherwise underperformed, he was restricted to the Fort and could be required to participate in extra close-order drill and other prescribed activities. Of the 11 weekends available for leave (the 12th was graduation weekend), I was restricted to the post for all but two. This resulted from numerous small infractions, and my natural aversion to intense regimentation.

For the two unrestricted weekends my classmate and fraternity brother Jack Chesley and I were houseguests of Mr. and Mrs. David Craig. The Craigs, "Uncle" Dave and "Aunt" El, had been neighbors and close friends of my family in Pittsburgh. Mr. Craig had accepted a high position in the national trade association for department stores and the Craigs had moved to a large and exquisitely furnished home in a lovely section of northwest Washington. For these free weekends, Jack and I both wanted lots of rest, a long shower, plenty of good food — all the comforts that a fine home could provide.

The Craigs treated us like returning prodigal sons. We were greeted cordially and informally, and were given time to scrub ourselves clean with lots of hot water for the first time in weeks, shave, and enjoy luxurious towels. We then sat before a roaring wood fire, and caught up on all the gossip. After a gourmet dinner, we collapsed for an undisturbed 12-hour sleep in silken sheets. Sunday was more of the same, with a special brunch and more leisurely camaraderie in front of the fire. It was difficult indeed to return to Fort Belvoir. (At our 50th Carnegie Tech reunion in 1993, Jack and I met for the first time in years. The first and principal thing we talked about were those heaven-sent weekends with the Craigs.)

On March 31, 1943 the successful candidates graduated from Officer Candidate School. Those of us from expedited ROTC programs were then sworn into the United States Armed Forces. We all were commissioned as Second Lieutenants and received our orders for our first assignment. The bulk of our class was assigned to Engineer Aviation Battalions. These included the 1875th at McChord Field, Washington, my assignment; the 1885th, 1886th, and 1887th at March Field, California; and the 1888th at MacDill Field, Florida. Jack Chesley and another Carnegie Tech fraternity brother of mine,

GRADUATION EXERCISES

TWENTY-SIXTH COURSE

ENGINEER OFFICER CANDIDATES

ENGINEER SCHOOL, UNITED STATES ARMY
FORT BELVOIR, VIRGINIA
11:00 A. M., WEDNESDAY, MARCH 31, 1943
POST THEATRE NO. 2

PROGRAM

Introduction . . . . . BRIGADIER GENERAL ROSCOE C. CRAWFORD
Commandant, The Engineer School

Presentation of Diplomas and
Commissions . . . BRIGADIER GENERAL RAYMOND G. MOSES
Assistant Chief of Staff, G-4

Administration of Oath
of Office . . . . MAJOR JOSEPH M. PLANT
Adjutant, The Engineer School

Benediction . . . . CHAPLAIN EARL O. PEARMAN

Music . . . . 31ST ENGINEER BAND

2387—FORT BELVOIR, VA.—3-23-43—1800

Bob McCutcheon, were assigned to the 1888th. The primary function of engineer aviation battalions was to construct airbases and their supporting facilities.

In retrospect, the expediting of our senior year at Carnegie Tech was a distinct benefit. We certainly learned and were challenged more in the 12 weeks at OCS than would have been possible in two weeks of ROTC summer camp. The rigorous conditioning at OCS started us well on the way to the high level of physical fitness we would need for overseas duty.

The Engineer Officer Candidate Course
The Engineer School
January 7, 1943 to March 31, 1943

Subject	Hours	Subject	Hours
Infantry Weapons	50	Obstacles	12
Map Reading	36	Command & Orders	11
Floating Bridges	29	Roads	11
Fixed Bridges	28	Camouflage	10
Marches and Camps	26	Military Organization	10
Vehicle Maintenance and Heavy Equipment	25	Musketry	10
Combat Principles	23	Engineer Reconnaissance	9
Company Management	22	Law	9
Scouting, Patrolling, and Extended Order Drill	20	Water Supply	8
Demolitions	20	Defense against Aircraft	7
Field Fortifications	18	Defense against Chemicals	7
Physical Training	16	Hygiene, Sanitation & First Aid	7
Aerial Photos	15	Training Management	7
Close Order Drill	14	Pistol, Revolver & Carbine	6
Military Discipline and Courtesy	14	Signal Communication	6
Defense against Mechanized Attack	13	Traffic Management	6
Engineer Tools and Rigging	13	Rail Movement	5
Assault Tactics	12	Classification & Army Postal Service	4
Ceremonies and Inspections	12	Engineer Mathematics	2
		Interior Guard	2

World War II Travel in the United States

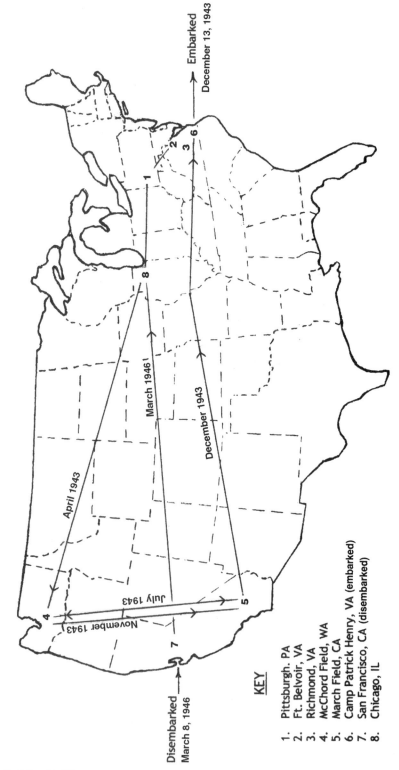

Embarked
December 13, 1943

March 1946

December 1943

April 1943

July 1943

November 1943

Disembarked
March 8, 1946

KEY

1. Pittsburgh. PA
2. Ft. Belvoir, VA
3. Richmond, VA
4. McChord Field, WA
5. March Field, CA
6. Camp Patrick Henry, VA (embarked)
7. San Francisco, CA (disembarked)
8. Chicago, IL

On-the-Job Training, In a Hurry

Upon graduation, many classmates were ordered to report on April 3, 1943 to the Heavy Equipment School at Richmond, Virginia for a two-week special training course. After Heavy Equipment School we were granted a seven-day leave and travel time to our permanent assignment.

At the Heavy Equipment School we received training in the use and maintenance of heavy construction equipment. This included bulldozers, diesel road graders, power shovels and rollers, rock crushers, ten-ton trucks, and Tournapull scrapers capable of scooping up several cubic yards of dirt in a single pass and moving it at 10 to 15 miles per hour to another location. We had an opportunity to operate all of these, but only briefly.

We were billeted several miles from the construction location and were transported back and forth in 2 1/2-ton GI trucks.

OCS graduate: Second Lieutenant William Collins King, April 1943.

The route led past an area of numerous tobacco warehouses where the tobacco was hung for curing. The odor of curing tobacco was very noticeable. On every trip it made me queasy, a hangover from my tobacco chewing misadventure at Fort Belvoir.

My seven-day leave was spent at home. I had a few dates with some of my Carnegie Tech former classmates, but spent most of my time with my family. These were treasured moments.

On April 24, 1943 I boarded a train for Chicago and there transferred to a troop train for the long trip to Tacoma, Washington. My father's parents lived in Chicago and we had in the past made several visits there, but I had never been further west. Having crossed the Great Plains, our train started the long ascent up the front range of the Rocky Mountains. At about ten o'clock one evening there was a loud bang and the train came to a jarring halt. A coupling in the middle of the train had broken; I was in the rear section. Only George Westinghouse's remarkable air-brakes averted a disaster. It was all downhill behind us, ten miles of curving track with steep banks rising on one side and precipitous cliffs dropping off on the other. It took hours for a maintenance crew to reach us and replace the coupling. In the meantime those of us in the back of the train got colder and colder. The steam hose had also been severed.

The trip from Chicago to Tacoma took about four days. During the daylight hours I kept my nose glued to the window, enthralled by the stunning mountain scenery.

On April 29 we arrived at McChord Field, an adjunct to the huge Fort Lewis Army base just southeast of Tacoma. We were an early cadre of officers and enlisted men assigned to the newly formed 1875th Engineer Aviation Battalion. Our training would enable us to function both as a general construction unit and as combat engineers. The battalion's full compliment of personnel included 33 officers and 777 enlisted men. These were allocated among the battalion's headquarters and supply company (H&S Company) and the three line, or letter, companies, A, B, and C.

I was assigned as the leader of the 1st Platoon of Company A. Our job was to develop effective noncommissioned officers to lead the platoon, and to bring the entire unit to a high degree of proficiency for construction or combat assignments. I made a decision to be strict, to strive for perfection, and to scrutinize the details, but to be fair. This approach was influenced by the relative freedom the enlisted men had during the evenings and weekends, when they could leave the base and enjoy all the community had to offer.

We had daily, rigorous calisthenics. There was extensive weapons training, including qualifying for carbine, pistol and M-1 rifle proficiency, and training with automatic weapons. I qualified as a sharpshooter with both the 45-caliber service pistol and the M-1 rifle. All of us participated in an infantry infiltration course. This included crawling on our stomachs, with rifle and full pack, through barbed wire entanglements with machine guns firing live ammunition two feet above the ground. The machine guns were sandbagged in place so they couldn't fire low. It was essential for each participant to keep his head and stomach close to the ground.

There were many construction projects, including building a rail spur into McChord Field, constructing a perimeter road around the field, camouflaging an antiaircraft and radar station 240 miles away at Neah Bay on the northwest tip of the Olympic Peninsula, and building a bridge over the boulder-strewn, rushing Nisqually River.

One assignment involved obtaining a field water-filtration unit from a warehouse in Fort Lewis, bringing it to our training area in McChord Field, and instructing the men of my platoon on its operation. The warehouse was open weekdays from 9:00 a.m. until 5:00 p.m. One afternoon I got four enlisted men and a truck and drove to the warehouse. The civilian warehouse clerk there was closing the doors for the day. I told him it was 15 minutes before closing. He continued to shut the doors. I was furious. He wanted us to make another 15 to 20 mile round trip, wasting gasoline, and disrupting our schedule for the next day. I spun around, called to two of the men to grab their rifles and come on the double. In seconds they were beside us. I told them to make sure no one, including the clerk, interfered until we had finished. They blocked the clerk's path, and pushed the door open. The other two men and I obtained and loaded onto the truck all we needed. I did not know whether or not I had the authority to take such action, but felt the clerk was not likely to report the incident for fear of losing his job.

From July 4 to 16 several other battalion officers and I were assigned to the March Field, California Camouflage School in the desert near Riverside. During the course we visited a large war production plant in the Los Angeles area. It was so well camouflaged that when we stood on the roof we could not tell where the roof stopped and where the surrounding town started. The summer heat there was intense. I was very fortunate to have been assigned to the much more temperate McChord Field following OCS. The Officers Club in the nearby Riverside Inn was delightful. On the two weekends several of us took in the attractions of Hollywood — the wartime Hollywood — and the delightful and then unspoiled ethnic markets of Olvera Street.

Back at McChord we also took advantage of the weekends. On one I rode a ferry in cold, wet, misty weather to Victoria, British Columbia. We took several trips to nearby and spectacular Mount Ranier. On one of my Seattle trips I met a former Carnegie Tech classmate, Lieutenant E. Hill Turnock. He asked me if I wanted to see something interesting. I said "sure." He took me to a complex of large buildings in south Seattle. It was in the evening and quite dark. There was high security around the area, but Hill had a pass. We entered a huge building, brightly lit, and I stopped dead in

Second Lieutenant King on an excursion to Victoria, British Columbia, October 1943.

my tracks. We were looking at an airplane far larger than any I had ever seen: a huge bomber that towered over us and extended to the far reaches of the building. I told Hill it would never fly; it seemed too big to get off the ground. It was one of the first B-29s to be produced.

In October a group of inspectors visited the battalion and put us through an extensive list of tests, apparently to determine whether the battalion was ready for overseas assignment. During the tests there was an interesting incident. My platoon was being examined on its ability to lay railroad tracks. The inspector wanted to see how well we could drive spikes through the tie plates that clamp the rails to the wooden ties. This involves a special sledgehammer with a long straight wooden handle and a cylindrical steel head about two inches in diameter on either end, widening only slightly toward the middle. This permits the user, known as a gandy dancer, to drive spikes close to the rail. The inspector picked up the sledgehammer and carefully looked over the men in the platoon. Instantly every man in the platoon used his most powerful extrasensory thought waves beaming "Rost, Rost" directly at the inspector. It worked. The sledgehammer was handed to Sergeant Myron Rost. He was one of my squad leaders, a tall, lanky, unassuming farm lad from Missouri who had spent his spare time working as a gandy dancer on the railroads there. We had marveled at his skill when we built the rail spur into McChord Field.

Sergeant Rost took the sledgehammer, stepped to the rail, set his stance with his feet apart and the right one slightly back. His swing was a thing of beauty. The sledge head rose rhythmically and continuously, first over his right shoulder, down striking the spike squarely, rising without hesitation over his left shoulder, down again to the spike and repeating the modified figure-eight path of the sledgehammer's steel head with no change in pace and no let-up. In seconds the spike was driven fully and cleanly home. We had just seen a superb performance by a master artist. The inspector shook his head in awe. He wondered aloud how it happened that out of all the men in the platoon he had to pick the expert. The platoon held its breath, then heaved a collective sigh of relief when the inspector walked on. He was man enough not to hand the sledgehammer to someone else.

We easily passed all of the tests. I was told that my platoon had the highest rating of any line platoon in the battalion, but my personal rating was average. The inspectors were surprised when they learned that I had been the only officer the platoon had had.

In early November Lieutenant Colonel Lavonne E. Cox was assigned as battalion commander and we prepared to move to March Field, California. I left the Northwest with regret and fond memories. The climate and scenery had been outstanding, the people gracious and friendly, and our food excellent. I had bulked up from a six-foot one-inch 129-pound sedentary student to 165 pounds of solid muscle. The battalion left McChord Field on November 3 by train and arrived at March Field on November 6, 1943. We were joined there by Captain Vincent N. Burnhart, Battalion Executive Officer, and Captain H. E. M. Stevenson, Battalion Planning and Operations Officer, S-3. We plunged into the many steps required to prepare for overseas shipment, including marking all of our shipping crates for embarkation from the Port of Wilmington, California. Without prior notice, our orders were changed to read shipment out of Camp Patrick Henry, Virginia. There ensued a hectic effort to readdress all of our equipment and shipping crates.

I called my parents and said that if they could they should visit me as soon as possible. They asked if Christmas was OK and I replied, "No." Obtaining railroad tickets was very difficult during the war, but my father was a very persistent and resourceful man. I made reservations for them at the Riverside Inn near March Field for late November and we had three grand days together.

On November 29 our battalion boarded two trains for the East Coast. Headquarters and A Companies comprised one train and B and C Companies the second. The route led through northern Arizona and New Mexico. Daily the trains would stop for a rest and exercise period of perhaps one half-hour. This was usually in a small, sleepy, out-of-the-way village or town. One such stop was the hometown of one of our enlisted men. He was overjoyed. He hailed a taxi, sent it to his home to pick up his wife and bring her to the train. When the cab returned, the soldier jumped in the back seat with his wife and had the cab drive round and round the block. When it was time to reboard the train we hailed the cab so the soldier would not be Absent Without Leave (AWOL), a serious offense.

At another such town there was a small saloon near the station. As soon as it was spotted, a tornado of GIs exploded through the saloon's swinging doors, swept up every bottle of beer and liquor in the place, threw more than enough money on the counter, and disappeared back to the train as fast as it had come, leaving a speechless bartender and two local customers.

Without further incident we arrived at Camp Patrick Henry, Virginia on December 5. There we were restricted to the base and just sat around waiting for our overseas shipment. One of the men in my platoon was a native of the area and had no trouble going back and forth between the base and his home. His security was assured, since he always brought back several bottles of choice wine or liquor for his comrades.

Opposite: In April 1943, when I boarded the train in Pittsburgh for Seattle, my boldest conjecture could not have anticipated that my wartime odyssey would take me through Beverly Hills, California; Oran, Algeria; Musoorie, India; Calcutta, India; Ledo, Assam; and back to Camp Kanchrapara in Calcutta, as well as to many other places.

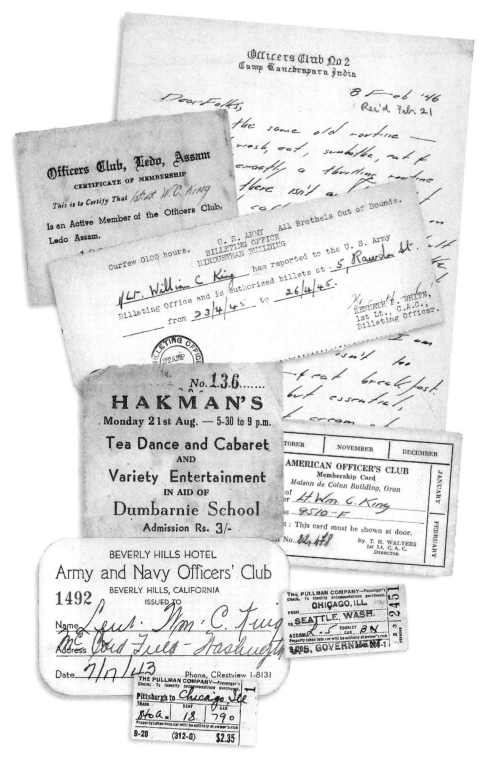

The Long Journey Overseas
For the 1875th Engineer Aviation Battalion
December 13, 1943 to February 24, 1944

SCHEDULE

Lv. Camp Patrick Henry, VA	12/13/43
Ar. Oran, Algeria	1/3/44
Ar. Algiers	1/15/44
Ar. Port Said, Egypt	2/1/44
Ar. Bombay, India	2/13/44
Ar. Dudhkundi, India	2/24/44

A Bang-up Start to a Long Journey

On December 6, 1943 Lieutenant Colonel Lavonne E. Cox and
Captain Homer E. M. Stevenson left for our overseas destination.
On December 13, Headquarters Company and Company A, under
the command of Captain Vincent N. Burnhart, boarded the USS
Huntington. Companies B and C, under the command of Lieutenant
Bender, boarded the USS *Tabitha Brown*. Both were Liberty ships, capable
of a maximum speed of only eight knots. We sailed under sealed orders.
For security reasons only Captain Burnhart knew our destination and
assignment. We were part of a large convoy, accompanied by mine-
laying ships, frigates, destroyers, and a couple of light cruisers. Air
patrols provided constant surveillance until we got beyond their range.

En Route

After a few days we slammed into a wild North Atlantic storm late in
the evening. Our ship was tossed around like a cork, with baggage
flying everywhere. Shortly there was a huge bang! Everyone grabbed
his life jacket and headed for the deck, certain we had been torpedoed.
Then came a second equally massive bang, followed by others. The
battalion safe had broken its restraining chains and each time the ship
rolled the safe careened across the deck in its hold and slammed into a
bulkhead. We had to wait until we reached smooth water before we
could chain the safe to its bulkhead again.

By midmorning we cleared the storm and the convoy commander reported all was well — with one traumatic exception. The USS *Tabitha Brown* with our B and C Companies was missing! It had disappeared. Convoy security precluded trying to locate it by radio. We had no way of knowing whether it had sunk, foundered, or just gotten lost.

The rest of the voyage was idyllic: lovely, sunny, warm weather in the mid-Atlantic, relatively calm water, frequent flying fish, and the fascinating phosphorescence of the ship's wake. As we approached the Straights of Gibraltar, we received word that the *Tabitha Brown* was safely in Casablanca, a port on the Atlantic shore of Morocco, and would join us shortly. We were jubilant. The *Tabitha Brown* had some-how gotten separated from the convoy in the storm and had had to make its own way across the Atlantic. Being unarmed and far slower than a German submarine, it was very vulnerable.

All eyes were glued on the fabled Rock of Gibraltar as the convoy steamed past. In the far distance we could see the great Sierra Nevada Mountain of Spain with its shimmering, snow-covered peak. On January 3, 1944 we docked at Oran, Algeria, and spent the next 11 days at a camp outside the city. The highlight of the camp was the bushel baskets full of the sweetest oranges any of us had ever eaten, before or since.

I had learned from letters from my parents that my mother's brother was somewhere in the area, serving as a Lieutenant Commander in charge of communications for a U.S. naval group. It did not take long to track him down. We had several memorable evenings at the officers' club in Oran. The local wine was plentiful but awful. It was great to get together, compare notes, and catch up on family matters.

On January 15, the battalion traveled to Algiers on a "Forty-and-Eight" train (during World War I, these cars were used to carry 40 men or eight horses). The train was an old wreck and in filthy condition. En route we were indoctrinated into the ubiquitous custom of children and grownups putting out their hands for money or anything worth-while and saying, "Gimmee bon bon, Joe." The war had left an already poor nation almost desperate for the bare necessities. At Algiers we detrained, and went by truck convoy to the Second Staging Area of the Center District, Mediterranean Base Sector, arriving at 10:00 p.m. There ensued a mad mêlée of 800 men drawing sleeping mats, getting tent assignments, and wandering through a huge encampment in the dark trying to find their tents.

Left: "Forty-and-Eight" railroad cars, en route from Oran to Algiers. Right: Stuffed like sardines into the "Forty-and-Eights."

The Staging Area was a huge tent city filled with transient GIs awaiting shipment to their permanent assignments. It was on a gently sloping hill high above the Mediterranean, very hot in the intense mid-day sun, and often near freezing at night. In the attempt to keep even minimally warm at night the GIs assembled all sorts of contraptions to burn whatever combustible material could be found. None of these provided much heat, but they were remarkably efficient at smoking up the tent so much that the occupants frequently had to dart out into the cold night for a breath of fresh air.

The latrines were several hundred yards up the hill and behind the camp. In the cold nights the GIs would huddle in their bedrolls as long as possible, then make a mad dash for the latrine. With increasing frequency they did not or chose not to get that far and relieved themselves along the camp street. In the noonday heat this created a huge air pollution problem. Camp officials solved the problem by having military police patrol the camp streets at night.

While waiting for transshipment, many of the U.S. personnel visited the casbah in Algiers, or went into Algiers in the afternoon to find a good French restaurant for dinner. One of the most popular places was the large cocktail lounge at the Hotel Alleti, Algiers' most prestigious hotel. There, at about 6 p.m., many officers and soldiers would congre-

Algiers waterfront.

gate, buy drinks for the French women who also congregated there, pick an attractive partner, and negotiate the price for an evening of companionship. I preferred to remain an interested bystander.

On January 24, our battalion boarded the British transport, the SS *Neah Hellas*, along with several thousand other U.S. personnel. There we met survivors of the 853rd Engineer Aviation Battalion. Their battalion had landed in Oran in early October, and sailed from Oran on November 25 on the British transport, HMT *Rohna*, as part of a 24-ship convoy. The next afternoon German bombers attacked the convoy. The *Rohna* was hit by a large radio-guided, rocket-propelled bomb and sank. Of the 1,981 Americans aboard, 1,015 died, resulting in one of the greatest tragedies in U.S. naval history. Earlier in November, the Germans had sunk four Allied transports, three naval ships, and two tankers in the Mediterranean.

The weather during our voyage was lovely and the voyage was uneventful, with one exception. One morning I went to the prow of the ship to enjoy the weather and whatever sights there might be. The only other individual there at that time was Captain Burnhart, our battalion Executive Officer and the ranking battalion officer until we were reunited with Colonel Cox. We chatted a bit, and I had an inspiration. We were traveling under sealed orders, and I knew that Captain

Burnhart was the only battalion member who knew what those orders were. We had been trained to build airfields and were heading toward the eastern end of the Mediterranean Sea. I had also seen the then secret B-29s in the Boeing plant in Seattle, and guessed that they must have an enormous flying range. Europe did not need such a range, but Japan did. Since the Japanese army had invaded China some years ago, China seemed an unlikely base for the B-29s. That left India, eastern India. So I said to Captain Burnhart, "It's great our battalion has such an interesting assignment." He was startled, but then relaxed and asked me what I thought it was. I replied, "We're being sent to eastern India to build B-29 bomber bases." He immediately became very angry, said that our mission had nothing to do with that, nothing at all, but then pointed his finger right into my face and said with all the determination he could muster, "And if you repeat what you have just said to anyone, anyone at all, I'll have you court martialed!" I replied, with total sincerity, "Yes SIR!" Bingo, I had hit the nail on the head. That episode was not related to anyone until the war was over.

A bit later I got hold of my platoon sergeant, Kenneth G. Kanter, a tall, broad, and very able young man from Wisconsin. I told him that I had been a hard-nosed, strict taskmaster during the training in the States, but said that was behind us. We had a job to do, we were all in the same boat, and it would be important to work together as a smoothly functioning team. I added that saluting me was not necessary except when senior officers were around. That relationship worked well and endured.

The *Neah Hellas* entered the Port Said Harbor in Egypt on February 1 and anchored there temporarily while waiting in the queue to enter the Suez Canal. Numerous peddlers pulled alongside in their tiny boats selling anything and everything to the GI's. One peddler held up a corroded, damaged medal, assured me it was very important, and asked a high price. For no particular reason, I became intrigued by the medal, haggled a bit, and bought it. It went into my keepsake trove and sat there for years until I accidentally learned the following story of its significance.

Late in the spring of 1942 the Panzer divisions of the Afrika Korps, commanded by the brilliant German General Erwin Rommel, had driven the British North African forces back through Tunisia, then through Libya, and on June 23 had crossed into Egypt. The British forces dug in near the village of El Alamein in western Egypt and temporarily stopped Rommel's advance. This area was bounded on the north by the Mediterranean Sea, and some 30 miles to the south by the Qattara Depression. This is a large desert area characterized by a jumble of hills, valleys, cliffs, and deep ravines, and is impassable for mechanized warfare. Nevertheless, the leaders of the Axis Powers were supremely confident that Rommel would rout the British, capture Cairo and Egypt, and move into the oil-rich Middle East.

The following is an excerpt from Daniel Yergin's epic and Pulitzer-Prize-winning history of the international petroleum industry, *The Prize*:

> Mussolini flew over to North Africa, accompanied, in another airplane, by a white charger, on which he planned to make a triumphant entry into Cairo. Rommel's goals were far more expansive: Cairo would only be a way station for a campaign through Palestine, Iraq and Iran whose final objective would be Baku and its oil fields. Their capture, in concert with the German forces then battling in the Caucuses, would, Rommel predicted, create "the strategic conditions" to "shatter the Russian colossus." Hitler was swept up by the same intoxicating vision. "Destiny," he wrote to Mussolini, "has offered us a chance which will never occur twice in the same theater of war."[1]

This grand vision was smashed by the British forces in North Africa. This is dramatically related by Hugh Gibson through the entries in his book, *The Ciano Diaries, 1939–1943: The Complete, Unabridged Diaries of Count Galeazzo Ciano, Italian Minister for Foreign Affairs, 1936–1943*:

> *June 26, 1942:* Our officers have prepared declarations of independence for Egypt, changes in government, et cetera.

> *June 29, 1942:* Mussolini has left for Libya.

> *July 3, 1942:* … a sudden and not unforeseen English reaction compels us to mark time before El Alamein.

> *July 6, 1942:* It is feared that after the impact of the initial attack is spent Rommel cannot advance further, and whoever stops in the desert is truly lost.
> … every drop of water must come…almost two hundred kilometers [120 miles] of road under bombardment of enemy aviation.

> *July 20, 1942:* At Rome. Mussolini, too, will return [from Libya] during the evening.

---

[1]Excerpted from *The Prize: The Epic Quest for Oil, Money & Power*, by Daniel Yergin. Copyright © 1991, 1992 by Daniel Yergin (New York: Simon & Schuster).

July 23, 1942: ... Mussolini ... is furious with the military, who for the second time have made a fool of him by making him visit the front lines at unfavorable moments.

August 31, 1942: Yesterday Rommel attacked in Libya.

September 2, 1942: Rommel is halted in Egypt because of lack of fuel. Three of our [oil] tankers have been sunk in two days.

September 3, 1942: Tonight there have been two [tankers sunk].

September 29, 1942: At this rate [of merchant ship sinkings] ... in six months ... we will have no more ships to supply Libya.

October 24, 1942: The British have attacked in Libya.

October 29, 1942: Another oil tanker sunk this evening. [In Libya] fuel, munitions and food are lacking.

November 4, 1942: A great convoy is being prepared from Gibraltar.

November 5, 1942: Libya front collapses.

November 8, 1942: American landings in Algeria and Morocco. This blow is absolutely unexpected.

In addition to preparing declarations of independence for Egypt, Germany and Italy had a medal struck commemorating this pivotal conquest and shipped a boatload of them to Rommel. This boat was sunk near the Egyptian shore by Allied planes. Apparently some of these medals washed ashore and one of them was the medal I purchased.

Two armored warriors (representing Italy and Germany) are pulling a crocodile (symbolizing Egypt) out of the Nile. The diameter of the actual medal is 1.2 inches.

Inscriptions
Left: CAMPAGNA ITALO TEDESCA IN AFRICA.
Right: [words eroded] DEUTSCHER FE [words eroded] AFRIKA

Our Destination

Later on February 1, 1944 we left Port Said and passed through the canal, stopped for a few hours at Suez, then continued on through the Red Sea, reprovisioned at Aden, and sailed into the Arabian Sea. The weather was clear and sunny, and the tropical nights with a full moon were spectacular. We would have been a sitting duck for a submarine, but there was none. On February 13 we pulled into the teeming Indian harbor of Bombay — just two months after our departure from the U.S. En route we had left five of our battalion in various military hospitals because of sickness. After debarkation, we were convoyed to a former Royal Air Force (RAF) camp in the suburb of Worli, India.

We had about a week to spend at Worli, so the entire battalion, in small groups, headed for the sights of Bombay. For one who had never been out of the U.S. before this voyage, Bombay was a miraculous experience. To provide a feel for my reactions at the time, I quote portions of a letter sent to my parents after we arrived in India.

> Bombay was just like an Arabian Nights panorama. Much of the city included modern, palatial hotels with cocktail bars, ultra modern apartment buildings, theaters, and first class restaurants. Zounds did we eat. A typical meal — a cocktail (spiked), hors d'hoevres [*sic*], some delicious soup made with cream, steak with mushrooms, fresh peas, French fried potatoes, plenty of bread and butter, some of the best coffee I've had in years, and a succulent desert. The steaks were the equal of anything available at New York's Waldorf Astoria Hotel

Gateway to India at Bombay.

Sahib Lieutenant William Collins King. *Crawford Market, Bombay.*

Taj Mahal Hotel, Bombay.

A typical Indian storefront in the native marketplace in Bombay.

in pre-war days — thick, tender and delicious. After starving on "C" rations and third rate fare, you can bet we made the most of it. The price of such a meal averaged about seven rupees, which in U.S. money is about $2.10. Not bad!

India is an immensely rich country. In Bombay there are stores of every size and description — from large fixed-price department stores to a vendor's small closet, only six feet wide and two feet deep. These line the alleys in the old section of town. They have beautiful diamond, ruby, and jade bracelets and necklaces. The jewelry costs a small fortune, but is much cheaper than you could get in the States. There is carved ivory, and ornately engraved and enameled brassware. Silver wire, like the finest gossamer, is woven into lacework. There are all kinds of precious and semi-precious stones — I saw some beautiful carved agate.

There is one section of the city with the native markets and their tiny stalls and booths. Everything you buy here you have to haggle for. The merchant starts about ten times too high and you start at nothing and meet somewhere in between. When we first arrived, the men didn't realize this and had lots of money. Prices rose tenfold overnight. It didn't take long for the boys to catch on.

These native markets would set you agog. They have everything for sale and lots of it is exquisite. I saw some glassware that beats anything I have ever seen. There are gorgeous silks and fabrics, ivory work, woodcarving, jewelry, and metalwork. All of it is hand made and it is fascinating to stand and watch the artisans work. They are wonderfully skilled.

The streets in this section are narrow and winding. There are millions of Indians everywhere — dressed in sheets, shawls, togas, and shirts and trousers of every color and description. And the smells — there is an infinite variety of odors of every degree of sweetness and putrefaction. Cows are everywhere in the streets, the sidewalks, the cart tracks, the parks. They go and come as they please and lie down where and when the spirit moves them. All cows are sacred to the Hindu; they can't be killed, but they can be used for milk and as beasts of burden.

On the streets a foreigner, especially an American, is practically mobbed. An Indian will walk right into a store where you are, take you by the arm and spout off at a mile a minute to the effect that you should come and see his wares. On the street, all sorts of scalpers accost you with knives, trinkets, etc. They also want good pens — $50.00 for mine — but I didn't sell. They want to buy good watches and rings. Two small boys will run up, one will grab you around the knees and the other will start polishing your shoes, working like a buzz saw. Then they want an exorbitant price. Often men will come up and show you a card that states they are certified fortune-tellers. One came up to me — a bearded turbaned old fellow with myriads of wrinkles and great tusks of teeth stained brown and red by betel nut. His hand was full of implements that looked like dentist tools, some had cotton wrapped around one end. He informed me that for a reasonable fee he would clean out my ears. I politely declined the offer.

After a week at Worli and Bombay we motored into the city and boarded a Grand Indian Peninsula train. It was barely better than the Forty-and-Eights we had ridden in North Africa. The cars were larger, but very spartan. There were two or three wooden benches on each side

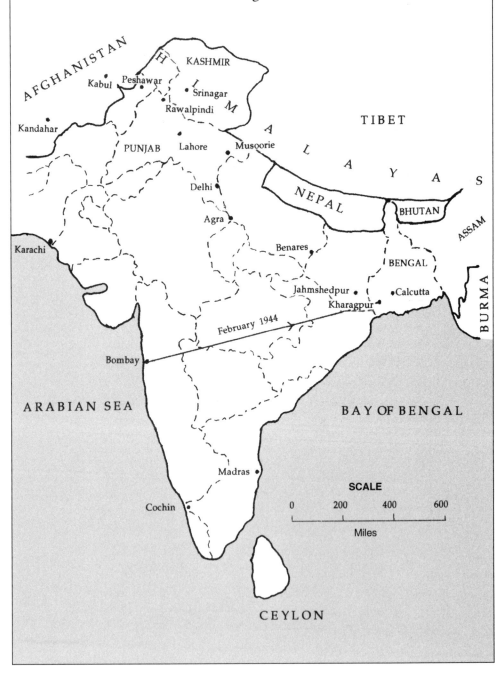

India
1944 – Prior to independence, and prior to the separation of Pakistan and Bangladesh from India

AFGHANISTAN

Kabul

Kandahar

Peshawar

HIMALAYAS

KASHMIR

Srinagar

Rawalpindi

PUNJAB

Lahore

Musoorie

Delhi

TIBET

NEPAL

BHUTAN

ASSAM

Agra

Karachi

Benares

BENGAL

BURMA

Jahmshedpur

Kharagpur

Calcutta

February 1944

Bombay

ARABIAN SEA

BAY OF BENGAL

Madras

Cochin

SCALE

0   200   400   600

Miles

CEYLON

of the car. They served as seats during the day, and beds at night. At the end of each car was a partial partition with an opening serving as the doorway. On the other side were the bathroom facilities. They consisted of two slightly raised, corrugated-metal footpads on the floor about 15 inches apart with a six-inch round hole in the floor between them. The passengers quickly learned to be prepared for sudden jerks and sharp curves. There was no water.

Our time on the train was spent observing the countryside, the villages, and the local customs. At every stop the train was besieged by pitiful waifs with outstretched hands calling, "No mama, no papa, Bahksheesh Sahib." I wrote home:

"Bahksheesh, Sahib."

All of the young children are naked and have swollen bellies from malnutrition. All the women have silver or ivory jewelry — rings on their toes, rings or diamonds in their nose, and bracelets. In the country the natives live in grass or mud huts. Their principal domestic animals are oxen, which they use for plowing and pulling carts. There are lots of water buffalo and stray dogs. The dogs are scrawny and mangy and act as scavengers.

Twice a day our train stopped at some village or town; we would all disembark and enter a local restaurant for our meal. It took remarkable courage to eat the food offered. Surprisingly the majority of us escaped without contracting diarrhea or similar maladies.

On February 24, 1944, two months and 11 days after leaving the United States, our train pulled into the little hamlet of Surdiah. This was located in flat, semi-arid, brush-covered country in the western part of the province of Bengal, some 80 miles west of Calcutta. We detrained, boarded our truck convoy, and traveled the few miles to Camp Dudhkundi — the first of our "final" destinations.

WORLD WAR II SYNOPSIS:
1944

1944, January – June
January: U.S.S.R. forces liberate Leningrad from the German siege.
        Allies land at Anzio, Italy; are pinned down there for four months.
February: U.S. captures Kwajalein and Enewetak Islands from the Japanese.
March: The Japanese abandon the Solomon Islands.
        Germany starts V-1 and V-2 missile bombing of London.
May: German defenses in Italy pierced.
June: Rome falls.
        D-Day, June 6th, Allies invade the Normandy beaches of France.
        Cherbourg falls to the Allies.
        U.S. invades the Mariana Islands.
        The naval battle of the Philippine Sea (near Guam Island) is fought. The Japanese
        naval force is routed.
        B-29s carry out their first bombing raid on Japan.

1944, July – December
July: General Tojo resigns as Prime Minister of Japan.
        The Allies break through the German lines in France.
August: Paris is liberated.
        Allies land in Southern France.
        The Japanese are defeated in the Mariana Islands; U.S. forces occupy Guam, Saipan,
        and Tinian Islands.
September: Antwerp is liberated.
October: The U.S. invades the Philippines.
        At the Battle of Leyte Gulf, the Japanese Navy is decimated; Kamikaze tactics
        are used by the Japanese.
November: U.S. B-29 Superfortresses start bombing Japan from the Mariana Islands.
December: The Germans launch a major, surprise attack in the Ardennes Forest in
        Belgium and Luxembourg — the Battle of the Bulge. The Allies are initially
        pushed back, but within two weeks stop the attack.

Building Nests for the Birds

At Dudhkundi Lieutenant Colonel Cox and Captain Stevenson rejoined us. Lieutenant Zimmerman, our battalion Supply Officer, was in Calcutta expediting the delivery of our vehicles and heavy construction equipment. All three had traveled by plane from the New York port of embarkation. Our battalion history states:

> Upon arrival [at Dudhkundi] we were all informed that ours was the task of constructing an airdrome capable of serving the new Superfortress, the B-29. The site was that of a former R. A. F. medium bomber strip. The job [was] officially known as Project No. 413. This was to be one of a group of airfields, all constructed simultaneously, to put into effect the *Matterhorn* or *Twilight Plan* of air-ground offensive against Japan; the western prong of a gigantic pincers movement.

This project comprised Base Section Three of the U.S. Air Force in the China-Burma-India Theater. For the duration of our work in western Bengal our battalion had been loaned by the Air Force to District No. 10 of Engineer Division No. 1. In January 1944, American forces in the theater totaled 95,000, including 16,000 engineers. By April 1945 these forces would reach their peak at 197,000, with 30,000 engineers.

The Dudhkundi Airbase

Dudhkundi was a remote site, located in a rural area, quite flat, but with scrub brush and scattered clumps of trees as far as one could see. We were housed in "bashas." These were bungalows, approximately 20 feet wide and 100 feet long, with a covered porch, thatched roof, one door, and windows. They had been built by a local construction group and were fabricated by building a bamboo framework and covering it with cement. We slept on wooden and canvas cots, and always under mosquito netting.

On our first night there we posted guards around the area. Shortly after dark native drums could be heard distinctly and the night was pierced with recurring blood-curdling cries — which we later found were the call of jackals. When the first shift of guards tried to enter their bashas to awaken their relief, they found the doors locked from within. So much for the bravery of these GIs. But like most GIs, they were resilient and resourceful. It was not long before they were joining the local villagers in their evening festivities.

The *Matterhorn* project included five B-29 air bases in western Bengal. Kharagpur, a town about 60 miles west of Calcutta and on a rail line, served as the hub. The other airfields were Dudhkundi, nearby Kalaikunda, Chakulia, and Piardoba. The task of the 1875th at Dudhkundi was to build and put in operating condition a complete airbase by June 30 — a mere four months away. The runway was to be 7,500 feet long by 150 feet wide, with four additional inches of concrete laid over the existing R.A.F. runway and a total thickness of ten inches throughout. Also included were a taxiway of 8,530 feet by 60 feet, 27 hardstands capable of holding 42 B-29s, 110 prefabricated huts, a Macomber Ordnance Building, three Butler Combat Hangars, control tower, operations offices, officers' and enlisted men's mess and recreation facilities, all the electrical, water, sanitation, and fuel-storage facilities, and a 25-mile access road.

The battalion had a few trucks, but most of its trucks, other vehicles, and all of its heavy construction equipment had been shipped separately and from another port of embarkation. Additional trucks were borrowed from the local engineering district. Each boat arriving at Calcutta with any of our equipment was met by one of our convoys to expedite delivery of the equipment to Dudhkundi.

An old R. A. F. firing-in butt (a man-made hill about 20 feet high and with a vertical front face) was equipped with hoppers at the top for sand, gravel, and cement, a truck-loading ramp at the rear for filling the hoppers, and four one-yard concrete mixers located at the front near ground level. Each mixer was provided with individual water

The Air Force target butt, to be converted to a concrete batch plant. Courtesy of 1875th Battalion.

connections and lanes for the cement trucks. Effective performance of this "batch plant" was crucial if our deadline was to be met.

During this period sand, gravel, and cement were stockpiled, a dam was built on a small, local stream, and a two and one-half mile pipeline was constructed for delivering water. Some 3,000 natives were hired to start the grading work. Seeing that the correct individuals were the only ones paid was a daunting job and involved fingerprinting.

Concurrently there were other tasks. From the battalion history:

> A few jobs had to be done while we were waiting. The District's siding at Kalaikunda was a busy place, it needed men to unload the daily freight trains — we sent them and took charge; breaking all previous records for quantity of material unloaded in a 24 hour period. The airfield at Charra required a 4000-foot by 60-foot parking apron of pierced plank — we laid it. Utility service roads were necessary at Surdiah siding — we built them. The hospital at Kharagpur desired several pre-fab huts — we erected them.

Night shift at the batch plant.
Courtesy of 1875th Battalion.

The native gravel crews. Photos courtesy of 1875th Battalion.

The native workforce building the runway at Dudhkundi, upon our arrival.
Photos courtesy of 1875th Battalion.

During one of the Kalaikunda train-unloading sessions, my platoon was involved in emptying a freight car full of large bags of cement. There was a waist-high ramp leading away from the freight-car door, with my men standing on either side in pairs. As the bags were thrown out of the car, each pair would grab the bag, and toss it several feet down the ramp to the next pair. This continued to the end of the ramp, where the bag was tossed onto a waiting truck. On checking how things were going, I noticed that the first pair at the head of the ramp was slowing the process. I replaced the smaller man and speeded up the tempo. No sooner had I done that than my platoon sergeant, Sergeant Kenneth Kanter, with a twinkle in his eye and a grin on his face took the place of my partner. The sergeant was a strapping young man who had grown up on a Wisconsin farm and outweighed me by some 65 pounds. The tempo increased further — bag after bag under the merciless Indian sun. Just as I was about to wilt and have to retreat, the last bag sailed out of the car. Saved by the bell. I said, "Good job, keep that pace up for the next cars. I have to get back to camp," and left with what dignity I could manage.

The first of our convoys bringing our vehicles and heavy equipment from Calcutta arrived at camp on March 29. Grading the runway with our equipment began the next day. Prior to this the grading had consisted of more than a thousand Indian women breaking large sandstone rocks into little ones with hammers. These were put into 20-inch diameter baskets by the women. Two Indian men would rise up out of the shade, lift a loaded basket onto the head of a woman, and retire to their shade. The woman would carry the loaded basket to the proper place on the runway and dump its contents. The Indian version of equality of the sexes.

On March 30 we wheeled out the first of our new, top-of-the-line equipment. Our large mechanized scrapers scooped up several yards of earth on each pass, carried them at ten miles per hour to the runway, and returned for the next load. Our graders had the area leveled when the next scraper arrived. The natives stood and watched dumbstruck. They had never seen, nor even conceived of such otherworld technology. They were also concerned about their high-paying (by their standards) jobs, with rates at 1.2 rupees per day, or U.S. $0.40 per day. That was not a problem. We had plenty of other work for them to do.

Left: Tournapull scraper with a D-8 bulldozer assist. Right: A roadgrader (left), a D-8 bull-dozer (middle), and Tournapull scraper (right). Photos courtesy of 1875th Battalion.

In April I was stricken with malaria, an ordeal I described to my parents in a letter home several months later:

> One night I was pretty well done in, but wasn't surprised because I had been working like a tax collector on April 15. But all night I tossed and turned, my back ached and I was burning up. In the morning the Doc. came over, took my temperature and in an hour I was on my way to the hospital — in the front of a dump truck with no cushions on the seat and over those turbulent Indian dirt roads. I died 16 times before I got there. They put me in bed, took a blood test — Malaria! For three days and nights I didn't know which side was up. I couldn't eat a thing and had diarrhea like no man ever had before. My head buzzed from all the quinine and Atabrine they gave me. After a couple of weeks I was chipper enough to start charming all the nurses, I was having a grand time, and not at all wanting to leave — so out I went.

Although I had had a severe case of malaria, I was fortunate never to have a recurrence.

Shortly after my return to camp, Lieutenant Cipolla, our adjutant, called me in, said I had missed the last pay period because of my hospital stay, and handed me a payroll requisition form to sign. Because I had little recollection of events during that period, and because I knew he had all the records, I signed the requisition. It was not long before the Colonel received a letter from the District Inspector General saying that I had submitted and received pay for duplicate requisitions in the same pay period. A number of itinerate pilots and some Army personnel had done this in the past and the higher-ups were cracking down hard. The Colonel, Lieutenant Cipolla, and I were summoned to the Inspector General's office. I knew the Colonel was fit to be tied.

I explained what had happened, and that because of my malaria I had little recollection of events during that period and so assumed Lieutenant Cipolla was correct in asking me to sign the second requisition. The Inspector General asked Lieutenant Cipolla if this were true. He paused and then replied "yes." My next pay was docked, I was not subject to any discipline, nor did I ever observe any adverse treatment because of this incident. However, it was included in my personnel file.

My Company A drew the assignment to erect the technical facilities and utilities for the new field. The first assignment for my platoon was to erect three Butler Combat Hangars. These were just big enough to get the nose and engine nacelles of a B-29 in either end. The hangar consisted of fabricated metal trusses with a vertical leg about 15 feet high, integrally connected to a sloping truss which ascended to the hangar's ridge line. Facing pairs of these trusses were aligned at about ten-foot intervals and the structure was covered with a huge canvas tarpaulin.

The hangars were shipped completely disassembled. The platoon graded the site, poured the concrete for the foundations for the trusses, and assembled them. The right and left trusses in a facing pair were each raised simultaneously into place by cranes. A man had to ride the free end of each truss up into the final position, about 30 feet in the air, so one man could put bolts through the holes in the connecting flanges and the other could put on and tighten the nuts. Since I never asked any of my enlisted men to do something I would not do, I rode one side of the first pair of trusses up and helped fasten them in place. The man I chose to ride up the other truss had been a structural steel worker in tall buildings before the war.

For the first hangar, the steel framework had been completed, all of the canvas roof panels had been laced together on the ground, and the entire roof tarpaulin made ready for raising by stringing the guy ropes from the panels up through pulleys on the roof trusses. This work was completed at the end of the morning shift. All that remained to be done was to have a crew pull on each guy rope to raise the roof tarpaulin into place and then tie down the guy ropes. This last step was the first task facing the afternoon shift. I visited the site just before the afternoon shift was to start, all was well, and I returned to camp. About one-half hour later one of the enlisted men rushed into camp and told me to come out to the hangar site, we had just had a disaster. When I arrived,

Raising the iron to the sky.

Assembling trusses at night — to escape the searing heat of day.

Both courtesy of 1875th Battalion.

the tarpaulin was torn to shreds and scattered all over the site, with pieces still attached to the guy ropes. I was stunned.

Just as the afternoon shift had arrived at the hangar, a large twister had torn through the area and started the tarpaulin whipping up and down. Some of the men tried to hold it down by standing on it, but were tossed into the air like matchsticks. All they could do was watch the tarpaulin disintegrate. I got hold of my men who had delivered the tarpaulin, told them to get back to the District warehouse as fast as possible to see if another tarp was there, and do whatever it took to bring it back. There was one and they brought it back. This one was assembled, immediately raised, and lashed to the hangar. Once lashed to the hangar trusses it was secure from wind damage.

The construction of the first hangar took three weeks. It took us two weeks to finish the second hangar and one week to finish the third.

While building the hangars there was an unusual incident. During the working shifts, I would periodically visit the site and check on how things were going. After each daylight shift I would carefully review the site to develop information for guiding the work for the following shifts. On one such occasion, upon arriving at the construction site after the end of a shift, I was surprised to see a small group of men from the platoon sitting on the ground; the balance of the platoon having

A completed Butler Combat Hangar at Dudhkundi, India.

Sergeant Louis G. Simon — one of my squad leaders and a very fine soldier.

already returned to camp. In answer to my query, they replied that the others had just overlooked them. It appeared that my platoon and squad leaders had not checked to see if all of the men were on the trucks before leaving the hangar site. So they all squeezed into my jeep and we drove back to camp. There I rounded the leaders up who had forgotten the men, drove them back to the hangar site, explained what had happened, and then had them walk back to camp to insure that this mistake was not repeated. There was never another such incident, and there were no ripples from anyone about it.

About 15 years later, when working for the Gulf Oil Corporation and living in Pittsburgh, I visited Akron, Ohio on business. My route passed near Aurora, Ohio, the home of Louis Simon, one of my squad sergeants in the 1875th whom I liked very much. On occasion, I would arrange to visit him at his home late in the afternoon, and we reminisced about our war experiences. During one of our conversations, he mentioned the above incident and remarked that the men had not been overlooked when the platoon returned to camp, but were the habitual slackers and had been deliberately left there in an attempt to discipline them. I immediately knew he was right; his explanation fit the attitude of some of the men left behind. When I asked why none of the platoon or squad leaders had mentioned this at the time, Lou just looked at me and smiled. I was shocked. I had flipped the tables and punished the good workers and rewarded the slackers. I had had a high regard for those leaders and at the time should have recognized that leaving the men behind was very likely not an oversight, but a deliberate and appropriate decision.

My platoon's second assignment was to erect a Macomber Ordnance Building. This building had an inverted "V" shaped roof, about 40 feet high, two side bays about 20 feet high with sloping roofs, and was perhaps 200 feet long. The center section was about 25 feet wide, and each side bay about 15 feet wide. The center section and the outside of the side bays were supported by heavy "I" beams. The entire building was covered with steel siding.

We also had a problem with this building. The heavy, vertical, support "I" beams were connected at their tops by other steel beams running horizontally between each two "I" beams for the length of the building. I designed special pulleys that could be mounted on the tops of the "I" beams so we could use our truck winches to lift the connecting beams in place. The first set of connecting beams was easily installed. The second set was more difficult. The third set would not fit between the "I" beams and we broke the pulleys trying to force them into place. We checked the length of the connecting beams and the spacing of the "I" beams. They were OK. We checked everything else and finally found that the bolt holes in each end of the connecting beams, used to connect them to the "I" beams, were one-half an inch too far apart. This meant that each of the first two "I" beams had to be deflected at the top by one-quarter inch. The third had to be deflected three-quarters of an inch, the fourth deflected one and one-quarter inches and so on. They just wouldn't move that much. An oxyacetylene torch was used to relocate the bolt-holes in one end of all the connecting beams. After that the building went up without incident.

On May 27, 1944 I was promoted to First Lieutenant, 14 months after receiving my commission as a Second Lieutenant at Fort Belvoir.

Shortly after the Macomber Building was completed, I was called in to see Captain Stevenson, the Battalion Operations Officer, or S-3. He told me I was in charge of electrifying the base, handed me a copy of the standard Electrical Engineers Manual, and told me to see the

Sorting out the mass of girders for the Macomber Building.

The steel skeleton, partially erected.

The completed building, with Lieutenant King in foreground.

Battalion Supply Officer to find out what equipment was available. I was nonplussed to say the least. I was a graduate Chemical Engineer and my entire electrical engineering background was a one-semester course. The Supply Officer said we had two large, direct current, diesel-engine driven generators, and to let him know about any hardware that would be needed.

On checking, I found that all of the buildings for the base were nearing completion and would include all of the internal wiring, fixtures, outlets, etc. That simplified my job tremendously. I was to see that each building was provided with the appropriate amount of energy from the generators: in short, to install the power distribution system.

I recalled from my electrical engineering course that direct current had the characteristic of progressively losing voltage as the distance over which it was transmitted increased. I pulled out the *Electrical Engineering Manual*, did some cramming, and calculated that we would have to order one-quarter-inch diameter wire. This would provide a 90-volt current at the furthest building. To provide the full 110 volts would require larger diameter wire, which would be impractical. We located the generator house so that all the critical services such as the control tower, operations building, and headquarters building would receive essentially 110-volt current.

The wire arrived in thick coils and was hard-drawn copper. Such wire is very stiff and hard to handle. It was tedious work to unwind it, straighten it, and install it along the pole lines. I requisitioned three excellent men from throughout the battalion, men who had earned their living as electricians before the war. They were put in charge of installing the two generators and the related control equipment. My platoon sergeant took charge of installing the wood poles for the transmission lines, the insulators, and the copper wire, while I bird-dogged the operation.

Before long, all was ready including several thousand light bulbs. The generators had been tested and were OK. Before the electricians threw the master switch, I asked if they had wired the generators to deliver 110-volt power. All of our electrical equipment was from the U.S. and was designed for that voltage. They assured me they had. I knew that there were two options for hooking up the generators: one would deliver 110 volts and the other 220 volts. I stressed this and again was reassured that 110 volts it was. When the electricians threw the master switch, there was an instantaneous, blinding flash; then nothing. They had made the 220-volt connection and we had just burned out *all* the light bulbs in all the buildings. Fortunately no communications or other complex electrical devices had been connected. Had I been prudent we would have installed only a few light bulbs before the power was turned on.

We were 10,000 miles from the source of supply so it might be a long time before we could get replacements. However, my resourceful noncommissioned officers found adequate replacements in the District warehouses. When this job was finished, over 160,000 feet of wire had been installed, feeding 2,500 outlets in over 200 buildings.

On June 20, the first B-29 landed at Dudhkundi. From then on they arrived daily. When a B-29, fully loaded with bombs and fuel took off, it became airborne by retracting its landing gear. The first pilot to do so must have been very brave. After retracting the landing gear, the plane would fly at that level until almost out of sight, when it would gradually gain altitude.

On June 30, four months and four days after arriving at Dudhkundi, our work was finished. The battalion had moved 720,000 cubic yards of dirt, mixed and poured 86,000 cubic yards of concrete, and installed all the buildings, utilities, services, and roads needed for a complete, operating airbase. The Air Force moved in and we moved out to a partially completed B-29 base at nearby Kalaikunda.

The battalion history relates, "The Division Engineer, Colonel P. F. Kromer visited us on May 11, 1944. His report to General Godfrey was one of straight-forward commendation. He termed the 1875th the best all-round outfit working on the western Bengal airfields. General Godfrey concurred."

George E. Stratemeyer, Commanding General of the Theater, awarded the Meritorious Unit Service Plaque "to the 1875th Engineer Aviation Battalion for superior performance of exceptionally difficult tasks and for achievement and maintenance of high standards of discipline during the period 1 April 1944 to 1 July 1944" (see the image on page 197).

On April 10, 1944 the Theater Commander had awarded "authority for all United States Army personnel assigned or attached to Base Section Three to wear one Bronze Star on the Theater Service Ribbon for participation in the India-Burma Campaign." This included the 1875th Engineer Aviation Battalion.

The first B-29 to land at Dudhkundi.

The flight operations line, including Control Tower, at Dudhkundi. Both courtesy of 1875th Battalion.

Dudhkundi Airbase — the operations (S-3) section drafting room. Men designing facilities to be constructed. Courtesy of 1875th Battalion.

A B-29 going airborne — hopefully. Courtesy of the U.S. Forces C.B.I. paper, *The Command Post,* June 1944.

Completing Construction at Kalaikunda

At Kalaikunda we were greeted with a morass of monsoon mud, British-style pyramid tents for our homes, and few of the amenities we had created at Dudhkundi. Back to square one. Kalaikunda was the base for three squadrons of C-46s involved in hauling aviation gas and supplies over "The Hump," an arm of the Himalayan mountains in western China and northern Burma. Because of the extensive and rugged mountains and the dangers of monsoon weather, flying over The Hump was very hazardous duty. Chabua, 40 miles west of Ledo, was the last airbase before reaching The Hump. It is in the northeastern tip of Assam, India, and is bounded by northern Burma to the south and western China to the east and north. Only 30 miles east of Ledo pilots had to thread their way between 8,000-foot peaks to the south and 15,000-foot peaks to the north. There were 19,000-foot peaks en route to their destination: Kunming, the capital of Yunnan Province, the south-westernmost province of China. Fog, ice, sleet, high winds, and Japanese fighters were constant threats. The terrain was so rugged and remote that downed planes were seldom located. These supplies were critical to the Chinese forces under Chiang Kai-shek and to the American Flying Tiger Air Force in China.

In addition, 60 C-109s, specially adapted B-24s, were scheduled to be based at Kalaikunda shortly. These, and the C-46s were especially hazardous since they carried full cargoes of aviation gasoline. A spark or bullet could convert them instantly into a detonated bomb.

When we arrived, the base included one 5,000-foot runway, a few pierced-plank hard-standings, and one Butler Combat Hangar. Our job was to extend the runway 1,500 feet, build a turning circle and a parking apron 3,500 feet by 380 feet — all suitable for use by the above aircraft. In doing this we moved 189,000 cubic yards of earth and, working three shifts a day, placed 37,700 cubic yards of concrete. Before the concrete

taxiway connecting the runway and the parking apron was installed, we received word that the C-109s would arrive in two days. We immediately started laying pierced metal planking to provide a serviceable, temporary taxiway. When this was partially completed, and well before the two days had elapsed, we looked up in the sky and saw the C-109s starting to circle the field! The battalion was instantly transformed into the counterpart of a movie, run at triple speed, of a colony of ants hurrying about on their daily chores. We must have broken all records for plank laying. All the planes landed safely.

While this work was being done, the battalion also installed, extended, and maintained power and water systems, added seven miles of access roads, and built two Butler hangars. We also put concrete floors under our tents.

By late summer, the workload abated. Many enlisted men and officers were given rest leaves to established British hill stations. Lieutenant Rudolph V. Tullson (Tully) and I were granted a leave to Musoorie, in the Himalayan foothills north of Delhi. We took a train to Delhi. This was a several-day trip. We were enthralled by the many peacocks wandering loose in the fields, by local villages and markets, but not by the Indian meals served in the railroad stations, our only source of food. From Delhi we were taken north by a U.S. Army truck. It was a wild ride. The driver sped towards and barely around ox carts, pedestrians, and animals. We spent the night at a small military post, Dehra Dun, at the foot of the road climbing to Musoorie. This winding, dramatic road was closed at night.

Lieutenant Rudolph V. Tullson (left) and Lieutenant King attired in informal uniform.

Lieutenant King with his trusty jeep in front of his tent.

Top: The batch plant at Kalaikunda.

Middle: Gravel supply to the batch plant.

Below: Pouring concrete for the Kalaikunda runway.

Photographs on both pages courtesy of 1875th Battalion.

Laying the pierced-metal planking.

C-109s, safely landed.

For generations Musoorie had been a retreat for the British from the searing heat of the Indian plains. They sent their children to the highly-regarded Woodstock School there. The streets were paved, there were comfortable hotels, attractive restaurants, and interesting shops. To the north we could see snow-covered Himalayan peaks. We were billeted in a comfortable rest house. It was a welcome change from the heat and humidity of western Bengal. Musoorie was comfortable but not exciting. The main recreation was going to a café in the evening, having an occasional drink, and dancing with English girls stationed in or visiting there.

Lieutenant King in the Himalayas.

On the return trip we left Musoorie a few days early. When we reached Delhi we arranged a trip to Agra, about 30 miles south of Delhi, where we visited the Taj Mahal. It stands in a formal garden with reflection pools and is absolutely breathtaking. It was built between 1630 and 1650 by the Emperor Sha Jahan in memory of his favorite wife. Nearby is the Red Fort, Sha Jahan's palace. The fort is a complex, royal enclave enclosed by massive red sandstone walls. Within are myriad and spectacular marble filigree screens, fountains, alabaster sculptures, and inlaid marble walls. There is also a small apartment with a view only of the Taj Mahal. Sha Jahan was kept captive in this apartment after his son had seized the throne. (Our trip is covered in more detail in the following chapter.)

Back in Kalaikunda, with the workload tapering off, we were able to do some exploring. I visited Jahmshedpur, or Tatanagar. This is a significant Indian city just 55 miles northwest of Kalaikunda, but a drive of three or more hours over winding, dirt roads. In this city is a large steel mill owned by the Tata family, a preeminent Indian industrial and commercial dynasty. The city had some good restaurants, and many shops and sights. In September, since there was little to do and we were prepared to move, I arranged with our company commander to have each of our four platoons take two days and a night off and enjoy an excursion there.

The battalion camp at Kalaikunda. Courtesy of 1875th Battalion.

In September the battalion received word we would be reassigned shortly. Among other related activities, we were to turn in to a central motor pool any of our trucks that were worn out or in poor condition. They were to be replaced with new equipment. I was in charge of leading that convoy for our company. The road led through countryside and a significant village before reaching the motor pool. I knew that road. To avoid problems by taking the convoy through the village, the Military Police requested us to meet one of their guides at 7 a.m. at a checkpoint prior to reaching the village, and to follow him via a back route, a route I did not know.

At 7 a.m. on the scheduled morning we had the convoy at the checkpoint. But no military police guide was there. After one-half hour it was clear that we should proceed, since we had to deliver the convoy and get back to camp that day. I was not about to take the convoy the back way and get lost in the countryside, so we followed our familiar route. In driving through the village, I carefully kept my speed below the posted speed limit, since the back of a convoy always experienced holdups and then has to speed to catch up. Before we got through the village an irate military policeman sped up in his jeep and lectured me for flagrantly disobeying orders. I listened until he was through and calmly told him that we had followed orders, but no guide had showed up so we had no choice but to proceed along the route we knew. He didn't believe me. I told him to check with any man in the convoy, and to identify the military policeman who was to be at the checkpoint. He glowered and, saying "Follow me," led us to the motor pool.

Lieutenant King's platoon leaders (back row, left to right): Sergeant Louis G. Simon, Sergeant Green, Sergeant Myron Rost. Front row (left to right): Corporal John Sobieski, Platoon Sergeant Kenneth G. Kanter, and Corporal S. Walker.

In the early afternoon of September 28 the battalion received orders to proceed to Ledo, Assam, the most northeasterly tip of India, tucked between the Himalayas and the Burmese border. We were to start moving out the next day. We were well prepared, so that should not have been a problem. However a sizable contingent of the men in our Company A had taken off that morning for an overnight rest and relaxation junket to Jahmshedpur. Since I was the officer most familiar with the road, I was given the task of bringing them back in time to ensure they were not left behind. At 5:30 p.m. I jumped into my jeep and raced the 55 miles to Jahmshedpur over the bumpy dirt roads, arriving well after dark. We had to round up all the men, which was very difficult for they had spread throughout the town, and get them in the trucks and return to camp. We had to get back in time to leave with the battalion or a lot of us would be AWOL.

On the return trip I alternately led the convoy, then pulled off to the side to count the passing trucks to ensure that none had broken down. It was then necessary to speed past the convoy to again lead the way. On one such dash an MP appeared out of nowhere, stopped me, charged me with driving well over the speed limit, and said he would file a citation against me. I told him the battalion had been ordered to move out later that day (it then being in the early morning hours) and my orders were to bring the men back before the battalion left. I added he could do what he wanted to, but my orders had to be followed. I took off, completely disregarding the speed limit to catch up with the convoy. We arrived back in camp at 4:30 a.m. This was one tired group that shipped out with the battalion a few hours later.

After some weeks our battalion Commander received a letter from the office of the Commanding General referring to the speeding citation and requesting to be informed of any disciplinary action. The battalion Commander replied, noting that the citation related to a nighttime trip when there was essentially no other traffic and that I had been complying with orders to meet an urgent deadline.

B-29 Missions from India and from India to Chengtu

SCALE:
One inch equals 550 miles

The Birds from Hell

When we left western Bengal for Ledo, Assam in late September 1944, our relationship with the massive B-29 effort ended. However, the B-29s were a key factor in the defeat of Japan. While a number of fine books[1] have been written about their role, it is still little understood and appreciated. That role is summarized in this chapter.

In the late 1930s there were some visionaries in the U.S. Army Air Force and in the American aviation industry who recognized the need for a very long-range bomber, one with a range far greater than that of the B-17 Flying Fortress. Preliminary designs for such a plane had advanced enough by September 1940 that the Army Air Corps signed contracts with the Boeing and Consolidated aircraft companies for each to produce a prototype plane. In May 1941 engineering drawings were essentially completed. The pressure to expedite production of such a plane was so great that, rather than wait for prototypes to be produced and tested, the Air Corps signed a contract in June with Boeing for 14 of their B-29 Superfortresses. In September the order was increased to 250 planes.

The B-29 Superfortress was a massive plane, 99 feet long, with a wingspan of 141 feet, a tail rudder as high as a three-story building, and a range of 1,800 miles one-way. A B-29 was capable of carrying ten tons

[1]Morrison, Wilbur H., *Birds from Hell, History of the B-29*. Wheeler, Keith and the editors of Time-Life Books, *Bombers Over Japan – World War II*.
Editor's note: the insignia above is that of the 20th Air Force (20th Bomber Command).

of bombs, and of flying at 30,000 feet above sea level. It had a top speed of 357 miles per hour and a fully loaded weight of 142,000 pounds.

By the spring of 1941 the Battle of Britain had been won; the German Air Force had given up its effort to gain air superiority over Britain and the English Channel. This secured Britain as a base for the future bombing of Germany. Such bombing was well within the battle-tested capabilities of the B-17 Flying Fortress and of the B-24 Liberator bombers. In addition, the B-29s would not be available in significant quantities until late 1944. Accordingly, the mission of the B-29s was shifted to the Pacific Ocean Theater where the distances from Allied controlled territory to Japan were much greater.

The B-29 was first flown in September 1942. There were numerous problems with the engines and the plane, requiring intense efforts in redesign and in production improvements. Wilbur H. Morrison, in his book *Birds from Hell*, writes:

> All new airplanes develop problems but the B-29 was so revolution-
> ary in concept that everything had to be developed from scratch.
> One by one the problems were eliminated. Even the pressurization
> system became so effective that this same basic system was still in use
> in jetliners decades later. The air position indicator … became the
> forerunner of the internal navigation system. The B-29 system was
> developed to navigate over vast distances, under conditions of radio
> blackout and overcast skies, where celestial navigation was impossi-
> ble. Many electronic, radar, fuel and safety systems … were devel-
> oped … by Boeing for the B-29.

In August 1943 the high level Quadrant Conference was held in Quebec, Canada. This included President Roosevelt, other Allied leaders, and their top staff personnel. At that conference the U.S. Joint Chiefs of Staff directed the Allied forces in India, Burma, and China to take the offensive in North Burma, and to build the Ledo Road from Assam, India to the existing Burma Road, thus reestablishing land contact from the Indian port of Calcutta to China. In September General Henry H. "Hap" Arnold, Commanding General of the U.S. Army Air Forces, had the schedule for occupying the Marianas Islands in the Pacific Ocean moved up to the middle of 1944 so airports could be built there and used by the B-29s as bases for bombing Japan as early as March 1945. This required that the Allied offensive in the Pacific save time by bypassing the less important islands occupied by the Japanese.

In October of 1943 General Kenneth B. Wolfe, commander of the B-29 Special Project, developed the Matterhorn Plan at General Arnold's request. This involved building the five B-29 airbases in India just west of Calcutta and four bases in Chengtu, in Szechwan Province, China, some 550 miles northwest of Kweilin (which the Japanese soon overran). The China bases were 1,200 miles closer to Japan than the India bases. On November 14, the War Department issued orders for a number of engineer aviation battalions to proceed to India to build the B-29 bases there. At the Cairo conference in late 1943, Chiang Kai-shek promised to build the four airfields in the Chengtu area.

My assignment to the 1875th Engineer Aviation Battalion and its assignment to construction of the India B-29 bases and later to the Ledo Road were direct results of these decisions made in 1943 for deployment of the B-29s and the campaign in northern Burma.

The distance from the B-29 bases in India to Tokyo was approximately 3,800 miles or twice the range of the B-29s. The southern part of Honshu Island, Japan was at the limit of the B-29's range when flying from the Chengtu bases; Tokyo was about 200 miles further. The B-29s flew fully loaded from the Indian bases to the Chengtu bases. There they refueled, flew to Japanese cities such as Osaka, dropped their bombs, returned to Chengtu for refueling, and then flew back to India.

From India to Chengtu the planes had to fly over "The Hump," a massive arm of the Himalayan Mountains, characterized by peaks as high as 20,000 feet, unpredictable jet streams, great storms, and often severely limited visibility. Until the Japanese were driven out of Myitkyina, Burma, their fighter planes forced the B-29s to take a more northerly route, significantly increasing these hazards. The greatest problem was flying fuel into the Chengtu bases. It took six to eight B-29s converted as fuel tankers to deliver enough fuel to Chengtu for one B-29 to make a single bombing run over Japan.

From Chengtu the B-29s had to run the gauntlet of Japanese fighter planes over China and Japan and of Japanese anti-aircraft fire over the targets. There could also be severe weather. The B-29s dropped their bombs from altitudes of 25,000 feet or higher. This resulted in low precision due to jet streams affecting the path of the bombs and often to poor visibility caused by dense clouds and fog.

The first B-29s, of the 20th Bomber Command, arrived in India at the end of March 1944. On June 5, 100 B-29s departed from India and bombed Japanese installations at Bangkok, Thailand. On June 15, 75 planes flying from the Chengtu bases bombed Yawata in the Japanese island of Kyushu. These raids inflicted limited damage on their intended targets due to engine problems, navigational mistakes, limited crew experience, and bad weather. The bombing raids increased in effectiveness as maintenance improved and flight crew experience increased. In August, Major General Curtis E. LeMay took over the 20th Bomber Command. One of his first steps was to relieve the B-29 crews from hauling aviation gasoline over The Hump. This function was assigned to C-109 transports, B-24 bombers converted to fuel tankers. In the following months the rate, size, and effectiveness of the B-29 bombing raids increased. The highest proportion of raids was directed at targets in Japan. Additional targets from India included Palambang in Sumatra, Indochina, Singapore, and Rangoon in Burma. From Chengtu additional targets included Anshan in Manchuria and Hankow in Eastern China, a major supply center for the Japanese forces there.

In June and July of 1944 U.S. forces in the Pacific captured the Mariana Islands from the Japanese. These included the islands of Guam, Saipan, and Tinian, all of which were some 1,500 miles from Japan, and therefore put all of the Japanese islands well within range of the B-29s except the northernmost island of Hokkaido. Construction of B-29 bases in the three large Mariana Islands commenced immediately. In February 1945 B-29 crews in India started transferring to the Marianas; the last B-29 mission from India took place on March 30. Wilbur H. Morrison, a B-29 navigator in the 20th Bomber Command, sums up their experience in the China-Burma-India Theater:

> Of the original 160 B-29s the 20th Bomber Command had sent to India, we had lost 147 in 1944 alone, and 30 percent of the crews. There were additional losses due to operations out of India in 1945 but at a much smaller scale. The command had dropped 11,477 tons of bombs, including a few mines, on 49 missions. Superbly trained, and forged in the crucible of experience, we were as tough and reliable as any fighting organization the United States had ever produced.

On November 1, 1944 the new B-29, *Deacon's Disciples II* and its crew, roared down a runway in Kansas and headed for eastern India and the war against Japan. Their route included stops on the east coast of the United States, Puerto Rico, Guyana on the north coast of South America, Brazil, West Africa, East Africa, Saudi Arabia, Karachi, and

Deacon's Disciples II *and its initial crew.* Courtesy of Lieutenant William H. Reed, Jr.

finally ended at the Dudhkundi Air Base in western Bengal on
November 15.

The crew consisted of:

Back row, left to right

William H. Reed, Jr.	Copilot	PA
Alton D. Fryer	Bombardier	GA
Robert H. Thatcher	Pilot	IN
Harold C. Snyder	Navigator	PA
Armon L. Jackson	Engineer	NM

Front row, left to right

Howard S. Heyden	Radar Operator	NY
Robert D. Paulson	Central Fire Control Gunner	OH
Lawrence G. O'Berg	Left Gunner	MI
L. Virgil Hall	Right Gunner	NM
Gale E. Furlong	Tail Gunner	PA
William G. Dodds	Radio Operator	PA

After arriving at Dudhkundi, the crew was assigned to another plane.
They flew six missions over The Hump carrying bombs to Chengtu,
and six missions against Japanese targets in Rangoon, Saigon, Bangkok,
and Singapore. In mid-May 1945 the crew flew to Tinian Island in the
Marianas; by the end of the war in August, they had flown 14 missions
over Japan. In mid October the crew members individually returned to

the United States and were separated from active duty. At that time, Reed was only 22 and the median age of the crew was in the low- to mid-20s. It is remarkable that a group of men so young could have mastered such a complex, difficult, and dangerous assignment, and done it so well. It is equally remarkable that hundreds of thousands of other teams throughout the armed forces performed as well. They were indeed a great generation.

On November 24, 1944 B-29s mounted their first mission from Saipan to Tokyo. They had to fly through a typhoon with winds ranging from 150 to 225 miles per hour. The high winds and 30,000-foot altitude resulted in little damage to the intended targets. On January 25, 1945 General LeMay assumed command of the B-29 operations in the Pacific. When reviewing the results of the B-29 missions in January and February he found that 5.7 percent of the planes had been lost in January and 4 percent in February. Only half of the planes had hit their primary targets and the bombing damage was well below expectations. He concluded the weather was a major factor, with adequate visibility often being limited to a few days a month. In addition, the almost constant high-level jet streams dispersed the bombs away from their targets. Also, bombing from elevations over 25,000 feet put a heavy load on the B-29s' engines, both straining them to their limits and greatly increasing fuel requirements at the expense of the bomb load.

To counter these problems General LeMay changed the flying elevation for night bombing missions to 5,000–9,000 feet. This eliminated the jet stream problem and greatly increased visibility. Fuel requirements were reduced, enabling a doubling or tripling of the bomb loads. Engine life was extended. Bombing accuracy rose from 36 to 91 percent and maintenance crews increased the operational time of the planes from 58 to 83 percent. Night bombing with incendiary bombs was used for urban targets. High-level, 20,000 feet or more daylight bombing was used for industrial and military targets where greater precision was more important. In March P-51D Mustangs, long-range, high-speed fighter planes, were stationed at bases on recently captured Iwo Jima, only 750 miles from Japan. The Mustangs provided fighter cover for the B-29 missions and flew their own strafing runs over selected targets on the mainland. Naval aircraft added to the onslaught.

The results were remarkable. During the next 14 weeks, 17 missions were flown over major Japanese urban centers. Each mission averaged

A B-29 flying over Japan north of Tokyo. Courtesy of Lieutenant William H. Reed, Jr.

almost 400 planes, dropped about 2,500 tons of incendiary bombs and experienced only 2 percent losses. The cities were ravaged by intense firestorms, with large sections burned to the ground, utilities and transport disrupted, industrial capacity damaged beyond repair, and casualties in the hundreds of thousands. Millions of Japanese fled the cities to the countryside and hills. Starvation and disease would soon become major problems. The bombings were continued, decimating the 66 largest cities. In addition, between March and mid-August 1945, the B-29s dropped over 12,000 mines in the shipping lanes and ports around Japan, severely reducing imports of fuel, food, and critical supplies. It is little wonder that the Japanese called the B-29s "Birds from Hell."

By mid-1945, the combined Air Forces of the U.S. had brought a once proud and powerful nation to its knees. The outcome of the war was not in doubt. Japan would be decisively and thoroughly defeated. The only remaining uncertainty was whether the civilian population would become so desperate they would capitulate, or would the military leaders force a fight to the death.

The atom bomb and the following unconditional surrender of Japan resolved the above uncertainty. But the 20th Bomber Command was not yet free of tragedy. After B-29 crew members had flown 35 missions they were generally given staff duties pending reassignment back to the United States. In September a B-29 was instructed to fly home to pick up and return with some special equipment. Thirty-five of the crew members who had completed their 35 missions were authorized to return to the United States on that plane. En route the plane made a stop at the Kwajalein Atoll. After taking off from Kwajalein it crashed into the ocean, killing all on board.[2]

[2]Morrison, Wilbur H., *Birds from Hell, History of the B-29.*

Typical Indian roadside shop.   *Starbucks' Indian precursor.*

An impressive village house with dung patties drying on the walls.

Exotic India

Most of the larger Indian cities had sections with attractive homes and buildings, and were beautifully planned and landscaped. These were the sections in which the British and well-to-do Indians lived and worked. They comprised less than 20 percent of the population. Here it was common to see four-wheeled horse-drawn carriages with collapsible tops. They were called gharrys and were very picturesque. Many had bells and it was pleasant to trot along in one on a nice balmy evening with stars overhead and the bells jingling. Occasionally we saw a marriage or funeral procession. The newlyweds, or bereft, rode in a gharry, followed by all their relatives, either in gharrys or walking. All were decked out in fine clothing and bejeweled. The entire procession was led by a group of musicians playing Indian music and dancing wildly.

The balance of the urban population lived in crowded sections of the city teeming with humanity and animals, and lacking many basic services and amenities. The streets were narrow and lined with small shops, many of which had workers in plain sight manufacturing goods with great artistry using primitive tools. For Americans these goods were quite cheap. Housing conditions in these sections were so bad that at night the sidewalks were lined with sleeping people.

In the rural areas the people lived in mud or grass huts in their villages. The huts frequently had patties of cow dung, shaped by hand by the women, plastered against the wall of the hut to dry. This was their major source of cooking fuel. The villagers were all thin. Most of

A village family and a typical village scene.

them ate only one meal a day of rice and maybe a few seeds or some fruit. The main meal was cooked in the early evening and the entire area would be covered by a pall of cooking smoke from the dung patties. At first I did not find this too objectionable, but after two years in India and Burma the odor of the burning patties became almost unbearable. Clothing consisted of lengths of dirty, white muslin. It was worn by the women in sari style, and the men wrapped it around their waists and legs in pantaloon style. The small children wore no clothing at all. Many had extended bellies, indicating malnutrition. Emaciated cows were everywhere. The principal domestic animal was the ox, used for plowing and pulling carts. There were lots of water buffalo and scrawny dogs.

The women wore silver or ivory jewelry: rings on their toes, bracelets on their ankles and wrists, rings and semi-precious jewels in their noses. The jewelry represented the family's accumulated savings; they had no other way of caring for it. The women did most of the work. They drew water from the well, collected the fuel, cooked the meals, cared for the children, planted the rice, and helped to harvest it.

Occasionally, small groups of our enlisted men visited the nearby native villages, especially when festivities were being held. During the Hindu New Year celebration devotees perform penance by having steel

Village beauties primping for the picture.

hooks inserted around tendons in their backs. These hooks are attached by ropes to a tall "May Pole," which is rotated so that the centrifugal force causes the men to be swung out into space, held in place only by the ropes and the hooks in their backs.

Photograph by Sergeant F. T. Monteleone, a field correspondent for YANK, *the army's weekly magazine.*

Left: The ubiquitous water buffalo. Right: Ox carts, the Indian counterpart of an "eighteen wheeler."

Our camp was located in the flat plains of western Bengal, about 80 miles west of Calcutta. Banyan, willow, and other deciduous trees were scattered around the countryside, and the ground was randomly covered with brush and brambles. Except during the monsoons, the weather was hot and dry, the ground semi-arid, and the sky cloudless.

In my March 16, 1944 letter to my parents, I wrote:

> At night you can hear the native drums beating and frequently jackals invade the camp. Their howl is like the eerie wail of the banshee — a mixture of wolf howl and hyena laugh. There are lots of lizards, scorpions, mosquitoes and snakes. We have to shake out our shoes and clothing every morning as a precaution against scorpions. The other night we killed a 5-foot hooded cobra behind our barracks. The natives were scared to death of it — even when dead.

Whenever we left our bashas after dark we took a flashlight and checked the porch floor before stepping out onto it. The concrete porch floors absorbed heat during the day, which attracted snakes at night. Any snakes were summarily dispatched. One night an enlisted man discovered a five-foot python under his cot and shot it with a pistol. In its frantic, dying contortions the snake demolished the wood frame of the cot. In addition to the cobras and an occasional python, there were kraits. These are snakes about two to three feet long and an inch in diameter; they are not aggressive, unlike the cobras. However, their venom is much more lethal. I do not recall one case of snakebite in our battalion. Snake bites were common among the native population, largely because they walked barefoot and often after dark.

Our camp was well-equipped and self-contained. We had showers

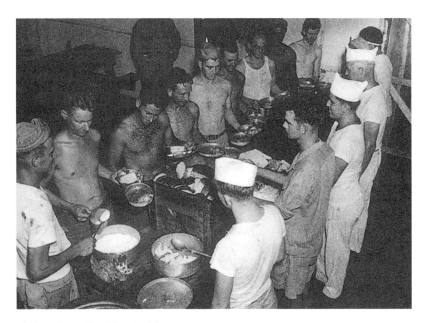

A chow line at Dudhkundi airbase. Courtesy of 1875th Battalion.

and outdoor latrines with sturdy wooden seats over a slit trench.
We had our own kitchen equipment and mess personnel, who were
tops. The food supplied was generally good. To minimize the occur-
rence of digestive ailments, we used little local produce. Most of our
food was canned or dried and imported from the U.S. However the
bread was made from Indian flour. By looking through a slice of bread
into the sunlight one invariably saw several dark objects about one-
quarter-inch long and pencil-lead thin. These were maggots, killed and
pasteurized in the baking process. Newly arrived GIs carefully plucked
each one out of every slice of bread; old hands did not bother checking
the slice. We purified our water with chlorine tablets in a Lister bag (a
large canvas bag suspended from a tripod with spouts on the bottom). It
had a distinctly unpleasant taste, but was safe. In the dry season it was
so hot and the humidity so low that we had to take salt pills to minimize
dehydration. I started out taking one salt pill each meal and quickly
worked up to six at each meal. Fortunately they did not bother my
digestion. Some of the troops could use only limited amounts without
problems.

There was another problem with meals. In that area there were many crows and kites, remarkably agile gray birds about the size of a blackbird. They are scavengers and on the fly could pick a dinner plate clean in seconds. When we ate in our screened-in mess halls, the birds were not a problem. At one point, the battalion Headquarters and Supply Company's mess hall burned down. While it was being replaced, the birds had a field day and the men had to be very resourceful to retain any of their meal.

In western Bengal's semi-tropical climate and primitive countryside, disease was always a matter of concern. In the spring, the hottest time of the year, heat rash was endemic among our soldiers. Although it was very uncomfortable and somewhat debilitating, there were no apparent aftereffects. In the heat, the men often were bare from the waist up when they worked. The wind blew dust against their bodies and they contracted ringworm from the contaminated soil. This did not pose a serious problem. The most widespread health danger was diarrhea. Regardless of how careful we were with our food and drinking water, it was hard to escape this affliction. There were times when I had so severe a case that my jeep was kept in front of my basha with the motor running, so I could race to the latrine and arrive in time. Malaria was the deadliest of the prevalent diseases. But our precautionary measures,

The enlisted men's recreation hall at Kalaikunda airbase — modestly decorated.
Courtesy of 1875th Battalion.

taking Atabrine pills daily, covering our cots with mosquito netting, using insect spray, and being fully clothed in the evenings, were effective in controlling it.

The battalion was self-sufficient regarding services and capabilities, but dependent on outside supplies. Each company had its own mess hall. The battalion had two doctors, a chaplain, a motor pool with broad maintenance skills, electric generators, and radio communications. We had a recreation hall for the enlisted men and one for the officers. There were electric lights in the buildings and phonographs in the rec halls. Natives were paid to pump our water, and do our laundry, tailoring, and odd jobs about camp.

Life for the American GIs had amenities. Mail service, including packages, to and from home was good. Officers received a fifth of liquor per month, the GIs a case of beer — and there were frequent exchanges. We had American movies once or more a week, and an occasional USO troupe (United Service Organization, which provided entertainment, travel service, and assistance to GIs). When time permitted, bridge and poker were played. There were two U.S. military hospitals in the area.

The officers and some enlisted men hired local youths as "bearers." Four of us had a 12-year-old named Goyahanna, we called him Joy. He polished shoes, made beds, swept quarters, hauled water, fetched ice from the mess hall every evening, and did any odd jobs requested. He was an engaging and enthusiastic youngster and very bright. We made him the talk of his village by taking him for jeep rides and letting him sit with us for some movies. A shared bearer cost me 12 rupees a month, or $4.00.

When we arrived in western Bengal in February, it was dry, the daytime temperatures were moderate, and the nights refreshingly cool. As the days passed, the temperature rose steadily. On May 13 I wrote:

> Now for the weather. Give me the nice cool breezes of Death Valley. The other day it was 112° in the shade — no shade — 126° out in the open air and the ground was 150° (we measured it). Imagine doing manual labor when it is 126°. I am burnt to a frazzle. There is no place to cool off. When the wind blows it scorches your face and dries your lips and skin. The sun beats down from 8 a.m. 'till 5 p.m. and parches your soul. Drinking water is always hot and tools are so hot that you can't even touch them with gloves on. Gloves wear out in a week. Truck fenders and hoods get so hot you can get a first-degree burn if you touch them. So what do we do? We eat salt

tablets, 16 to 20 a day, sweat and sweat more, and toss in the heat at night. We curse India. We have to knock off work between 11 in the morning and 5 in the afternoon and work 9-hour shifts from 5 p.m. to 2 a.m. and 2 a.m. to 11 a.m. We sleep at night out on the porch to catch any breeze. And it is only the middle of May!

During the latter part of the dry season vegetation dried up. Water in the rice paddies vanished. The dirt become as hard as brick and shriveled up, leaving gaping cracks crisscrossing the bottom of the rice paddies. In the heat of the day, nothing moved, not even mad dogs and Englishmen.

In late May the Monsoons started. There were sudden short-lived but torrential downpours. On May 27 I wrote:

It looks like the prelude to the monsoons. It has rained a couple of times in the past three weeks and when it rains it gets wonderfully cool for the next day or so, perhaps down to 95° in the shade, but that is heaven. When it rains it floods. In an hour of rain, so much comes down that everything is flooded for days. During the rain all the natives vanish. No matter what they are doing they just up and disappear. Shortly after the rain stops though, you can see them bathing and doing their laundry in a flooded rice paddy. They are quite modest and bathe with their clothes on or get into the water up to their neck before undressing. When they wash their clothes they soak them and then slap them down on a flat rock. The water is so muddy I don't see what they accomplish.

A do-it-yourself laundry in a convenient rice paddy.

Within a few days after the first rains, the rice paddies, which had been baked brick hard, were not only full of water, but were teeming with thousands of bull frogs and millions of insects. Natives were successfully catching small fish the size of bluegills with makeshift rods and hooks. I never stopped marveling at how such a profusion of life could spring forth from ground that had been so hostile only a few days before.

During this early phase of the monsoon the weather was characterized by violent fronts that would blast through unannounced, last an hour or two, and disappear. Prodigious quantities of rain fell in a short time. At times the edge of the rainfall would be defined with incredible sharpness. On numerous occasions I would drive along the country roads with rain teeming down on one side, but with the other dry. Sometimes the wind was so violent that it rained horizontally. More than once this caused my jeep to stall. So much water was blown into the engine that it shorted out the electrical system. I would just have to sit there until it dried.

The sunsets were glorious. Evening after evening the sky was filled with high, fleecy clouds ablaze with brilliant rainbow hues. The sunsets lasted, reflecting the changing color of the setting sun. They were a pure joy. Never since have I seen so many gorgeous sunsets over a continuing period.

We enjoyed another spectacular natural phenomenon. I wrote on June 9:

> Often in the evening we see what may be a southern sequel to the Northern Lights. In reality it is heat lightning. A great cloud bank will become supercharged and huge bolts of lightning will lash out against the black sky, or will rip through the clouds, lighting up the entire bank like a massive wad of cotton against black velvet. It is breathtaking — and all without a sound except the gentle whisper of the wind in the trees.

In midsummer the violent weather fronts were replaced by slow moving ones which deluged us with steady rain. By late June the monsoon came in earnest. It rained steadily and unremittingly for hours, day after day. Our clothes, bedding, and tent canvas were continually and depressingly damp. The temperature hovered in the 90's and the humidity stayed close to 100 percent, but this was far better than the searing spring heat.

Our First Leave

In early August 1944, Lieutenant Tullson (Tully) and I traveled from Kalaikunda about 70 miles to Calcutta, one of India's largest cities. It had the largest population of destitute people of any Indian city, but like all Indian cities, it also had its amenities. We stayed at the attractive Grand Hotel in a pleasant section of the city. One afternoon we went to the race track and enjoyed the festivities there. I bet on three of four winners, but only won 28 rupees ($9.00) because the odds were so poor.

After the races I was relaxing in the lounge of the Grand Hotel when to my astonishment one of my fraternity brothers from Carnegie Tech, Ted Fisher, walked by. He was 6'4" tall and weighed 230 pounds — not easily overlooked. I hailed him and we had a grand reunion. He was a civilian working for Hamilton Propellers and had spent the past two years visiting air bases in North Africa, Egypt, Arabia, India, Burma, and China. Ted knew that two more of our schoolmates were in town and the four of us had a grand dinner together, sharing experiences well into the evening.

That day Lieutenant Tullson and I had confirmed at the train station our reservations for Delhi, and they were all in order. The next day we arrived at the station an hour early, as we had been advised to do. We were not on the passenger list. No reservations! We could not find the American Rail Transportation Officer, and the British Rail Transportation Officer was peeved that the American officer was not available.

In my letter to my family dated August 13, I wrote:

> The two of us grabbed our luggage and hopped into one of the train's compartments. I looked around, four berths, three men already there. Two were English officers and one was an Indian. The Indian had loads of luggage and one English officer was in an upper berth. I looked at the other English officer (all the while we were moving our luggage in) and asked if he had a reservation for the bunk he was on. He said "Is this yours?" I said "Yes, we have reservations for these two," and he politely left. We hurriedly dug ourselves in to withstand any assault by the rightful owners, but none showed.

> The compartment was fair, stuffed leather bunks, and a small lavatory with bowl and toilet. Twice during the trip we had a fifth man, no other place to ride. En route we saw rice paddies, frequent peacocks, monkeys, cranes, a few camels and many villages. Every morning and afternoon we were served tea and toast at some convenient stop. For lunch and dinner there was a stop at a large town for an hour or so. We ate at a European-style restaurant (Indian waiters though) in the station. We got chummy with our English fellow passenger and usually ate with him. He seemed to know the ropes. We asked him if the food was OK. He shrugged and said that was the chance you took, though he had usually found it OK. So far there have been no ill effects.

A camel-drawn cart, picturesque but not common.

We left Musoorie four days early, since we had to return through Delhi and I wanted to visit the Taj Mahal in Agra — 120 miles south of Delhi. We arrived in New Delhi in the evening and spent the night in the transient officers' quarters. New Delhi is just across the street from Delhi and is a beautiful place. There are large palatial buildings of modern design, wide boulevards, parkways, beautiful gardens and landscaping. The seat of the Indian Government, the British Raj, is here. The architecture and landscaping of the government buildings is stunning, certainly befitting the stature of the nation. But you can also see camels meandering down the street, a convoy of bullock carts pulled by huge white Brahma steers, or perhaps natives trudging along. The place is very clean and there are any number of expensive shops where you can buy exquisite jewelry, star sapphires, laces, ivory, or pottery. I saw a superb, hand-carved, filigree ivory screen perhaps 5 feet tall and 6 feet wide for only 40,000 Rupees, or $13,000. It was part of a solid ivory bedroom suite which was priced at a cool $100,000.

We caught the afternoon train to Agra and stayed at the officers' club. For dinner they feted us with steak, French fries, FRESH fried eggs, toast and fresh milk. The milk was a bit sour. In the morning we took a tonga (a comfortable two-wheeled, horse-drawn, covered cart) to the Taj Mahal. There an Indian guide offered his services,

A small portion of the walls of the massive Red Fort in Agra. The entrance is at the left center.

and was quite a help. He asked if we wished to see the Agra Fort, "Of course" we replied. The fort is a huge red brick structure with two moats, a 40-foot wall and a 70-foot wall with drawbridges and battlements. It was fascinating. In it was the palace of Sha Jahan, the Mogul emperor who built the Taj for his favorite wife, Mumtaz Mahal. There were gem inlaid porticos, marble shrines, spacious baths with thousands of diamond-shaped pieces of inlaid mica to make a mirror fairyland, alabaster windows to let in the light but keep out the weather, and a huge stone bowl five-feet high used as the ruler's bathtub.

We then traveled the short distance to the Taj. On the way we passed some burning ghats or Hindu burial grounds. Here the people bring the dead to the riverbank, place the corpse on a pier of wood or dung (depending on the wealth of the relatives) and burn it. Three days later they return and throw all the ashes and bones into the river. If the corpse is that of a child under twelve, it is thrown into the river where it is devoured by giant turtles.

A funeral pyre in the burning ghats.

A tonga driver enjoying a deluxe shave outside the entrance to the Taj Mahal.

The Taj consists of four major units within a rectangle. At one end is the ornate and large entrance structure. On either side are two shrines. At the far end is the Taj with a long reflection pool in front of it. As we walked through the gate the Taj flashed into view. I just stood and looked in awe. It is made of white marble profusely decorated with inlaid designs of black marble and semi-precious stones. It is wonderfully preserved. In the main gallery on the first floor, are two exquisite monuments representing the site of the graves of Sha Jahan and his wife. They are enclosed in a hand-carved white marble, filigree screen, which took ten years to make and is a dream. The sarcophagi where the bodies are actually entombed are in the level below the first floor.

On the way back to the officers' club a peddler with a spiffy leather-covered walking stick accosted me. He pulled on the handle, and Lo, out came a 30-inch sword blade. I said, "How much?" He said "eight rupees," I replied, "four." He said "No," so I hopped into the tonga to leave. He said "four." I really didn't want it, but being a man of my word I paid him the four rupees and acquired the sword-cane.

We took the afternoon train back to Delhi and entered the officers' quarters just as the dinner hour was finishing, so we went directly to the dinning room, cane and all. While eating dinner, the Indian waiters gathered at our table, eyeing my cane. They suspected it was a sword cane, and I discreetly demonstrated that it was. They asked how much it had cost and I replied, "four rupees." They agreed that was a fine price. They asked how much they could buy it for: I answered, "50 rupees!" Thereupon ensued a bit of colorful Hindustan language. Finally realizing I could never use the cane or get it home, I said, "six rupees." They bought it for that. That was the first, and last, time I made money dealing with an Indian.

Back in New Delhi, we lounged around under a fan, ate good meals at a fine restaurant, saw some movies, and got ourselves invited to a swanky British officers' club where we went swimming in a beautiful pool and had a steak dinner. Rough life! We arose at 6 a.m., grabbed a luxury airliner (with a private library) to Calcutta and returned to camp by train and truck.

When we had finished constructing our runways, a form of entertainment was to take a few men in my jeep and drive after dark to the beginning of the runway. We waited until a jackal crossed the runway in front of us. When the jackal was in the middle of the runway I would turn on the headlights, start the engine, and race toward the jackal. The jackal invariably chose to run down the length of the runway since the headlights lighted the way. We drove within a few inches of the animal, shouted, honked the horn, and slapped the side of the jeep, making as much noise as possible. At the end of the runway we stopped and the beleaguered jackal would stagger into the brush completely exhausted.

Another diversion was to listen to Japanese broadcasts. In a letter to my family dated March 16, I wrote:

Quite regularly we get Japanese propaganda in English over our short wave radio. Boy, it's brutal. Every time there is an engagement, they turn it into a Japanese victory. They are always reporting dissention and jealousy between English and American officers and

Somewhere in India

Somewhere in India, where the sun is like a curse,

And each day is followed by another — slightly worse;

Where the rain comes down in torrents and the mud is ankle deep.

Somewhere in India, where the buffalo like to roam

And sacred cows wear halos as they wend their way back home.

Where the jackals nightly howling robs the sleep of every man,

Where the whiskey's made of brimstone and the beer's ten chips a can.

Somewhere in India, where the nights are made for love,

Where the moon is like a spotlight with the Southern Cross above;

It sparkles like a moonbeam on the throat of a tropic night,

'Tis a shameful waste of beauty, as there's not a skirt in sight.

Somewhere in India, where the postman comes too late;

Where a Christmas package in April is considered up to date.

Our pockets bulge with rupees, but we haven't got a cent.

We don't miss the money, as we couldn't get it spent.

Somewhere in India, where the snakes and tigers play,

Where a thousand skeeters gather to replace each one we slay.

Take me back to old Missouri and let me hear the chapel bell,

For this God-forsaken country is a substitute for hell.

Author: An unknown GI.

troops. They are constantly urging the Indians to revolt, and spread stories of atrocities by us and the English that make our stories about the Japanese pale into insignificance. Listening to them one can easily understand why the Japanese think they are fighting for the ultimate good of humanity and are winning the war. The Japanese civilians must have been shocked when the B-29s started bombing Japan.

By September the cloud cover became more moderate and scattered. The rains stopped, the sun drove the temperature well over 100 degrees, and a haze of moisture rose from the saturated ground. We lived in a steam bath, eagerly awaiting cooler winter weather.

The Rail Trip: Calcutta to Ledo

The Trip to Nowhere

When the battalion departed from western Bengal, the first half of its vehicular equipment left Kalaikunda by road at 6:00 a.m. September 29, 1944, and the second on September 30. A contingent of men from Company A and H&S Company accompanied the equipment. The balance of the troops departed by train at 10:00 p.m. on September 30. The troop train passed through Calcutta at 6:30 a.m. October 1 and continued on to Parbatapur, where we changed from standard gauge to a narrower gauge train on October 2. On this train I had my own cramped compartment at the end of a car. It had rough wood paneling, a bunk bed barely long enough for me, and a minimal washbasin and toilet facility. Each of us had been given a fresh can of insect spray. I was mildly surprised to see a broom in the compartment.

Shortly after dark (there were no lights in the cars), I went to bed. Before falling asleep I heard a rustling sound, and things began moving under and over my bed. I lit my flashlight, swung it around the compartment, and saw a seething mass of cockroaches covering everything and swarming everywhere. I grabbed the insect repellent and flooded the compartment with spray — so much so I had to force the window open and stick my head out to breathe. The rustling stopped. I opened the outside door, swept all of the dead cockroaches out, checked to ensure none had been missed, and went back to bed. After a short sleep, a second invasion of cockroaches awakened me. Apparently these had scurried behind the paneling during the first spraying. I repeated my counterattack, went back to bed, and enjoyed an uninterrupted sleep.

Ferrying the battalion across the Brahmaputra River.

Fresh pork en route to market.

A sword swallower and magician earning a living, Pandu Station.

The next morning we arrived at the ferry landing in Gauhati, north of Calcutta, detrained, boarded the ferry, and crossed the wide and muddy Brahmaputra River. The Brahmaputra originates in the foothills of the Himalayas on their northern flank in China, flows eastward to a gap north of Ledo, south through the gap and then west through Assam, along the southern flank of the Himalayas to Gauhati. Past Gauhati it veers south to Calcutta, and empties into the Bay of Bengal. After landing we walked to the British Portsmouth Camp at Pandu, had brunch, climbed back onto another rickety, meter gauge train, and departed at 1:00 p.m. Our train trip led up the Brahmaputra Valley and ended on October 5 at Margherita, a staging area just west of Ledo.

The vehicular and heavy equipment convoys generally followed the same route, but went by road. The road ended at Tinsukia, 40 miles west of Ledo. There the vehicles and equipment had to be loaded onto flatbed railroad cars for the trip to Ledo, since no road connected the two. On October 7, I received orders placing me on temporary duty, reporting to the commander of the railhead and marshalling yard at Tinsukia, with the assignment of expediting the transport of the battalion's vehicles from there to Ledo.

Late in the week I arrived by train in Tinsukia, met with the railhead commander, and explained my assignment. He was the officer in charge of the American unit which ran the railhead. I asked him how many flat cars he had and would have through the following week, about the loading procedure, and if priority could be obtained for using them. He gave me the information about the cars, but said it was necessary to get the authority to use them from the British Major in charge of the railhead. He added, "Well it's after lunch, the Major will undoubtedly be at the bar in the British Officers' Club." Using the commander's jeep, I found the club and the Major as predicted, introduced myself, explained my mission, and asked for permission to use the flatcars at the railhead. He asked how many vehicles we had. My answer was, "180 trucks and smaller vehicles." He gasped and said it would take months to transport all that to Ledo. I asked why so much time? He explained how slow and inefficient the operations were at the railhead. I said if he would give me full use of all the flatcars at the railhead for the next week I would be accountable for their use and the vehicles' transport. He shook his head with incredulity, but granted permission.

I returned to the railhead and told the commander about my conversation with the British Major. The commander smiled and observed that the British forces had very few and very old vehicles, so took great pains to avoid damaging them. This resulted in their slow rates for loading vehicles onto the trains. We worked out our procedures. Three flatcars could be loaded at a time from the loading ramp. As soon as loaded, an engine would move them from the ramp to the departure siding and a second engine would bring the next three cars to the ramp. A soldier was to be stationed on the end of the last car to help guide the loading vehicles. Drivers of vehicles waiting to be loaded would be stationed beside each car with "come-alongs" to chain the vehicles firmly onto the cars. The commander was most cooperative.

The first convoy section arrived Sunday evening. I briefed the GIs on the loading procedure, and emphatically told them of the need for both speed and safety. Our GIs responded admirably to the challenge. Company A started loading early Monday morning, finished shortly after noon, and the train departed for Ledo, returning unloaded shortly after midnight. Company B's and Company C's vehicles moved out on Tuesday and Wednesday, and on Thursday H&S Company's vehicles moved out — all without any problems. Early Thursday afternoon I borrowed a jeep, visited the British Major at the Officers' Club, and reported that all but the last contingent had arrived in Ledo and the last would be leaving upon my return to the railhead. He looked at me in speechless amazement. I thanked him for his assistance, saluted, and left. Back at the railhead I jumped into a jeep loaded on one of the flatcars and enjoyed the four-hour ride to Ledo, through a lovely semi-tropical evening. The town of Ledo turned out to be as remote and unremarkable as any spot in the world: it was nothing and nowhere.

Signboard at the head of the Ledo (Stilwell) Road: Kunming — 1,079 miles.

The Burma-Ledo Roads: Calcutta to Kunming

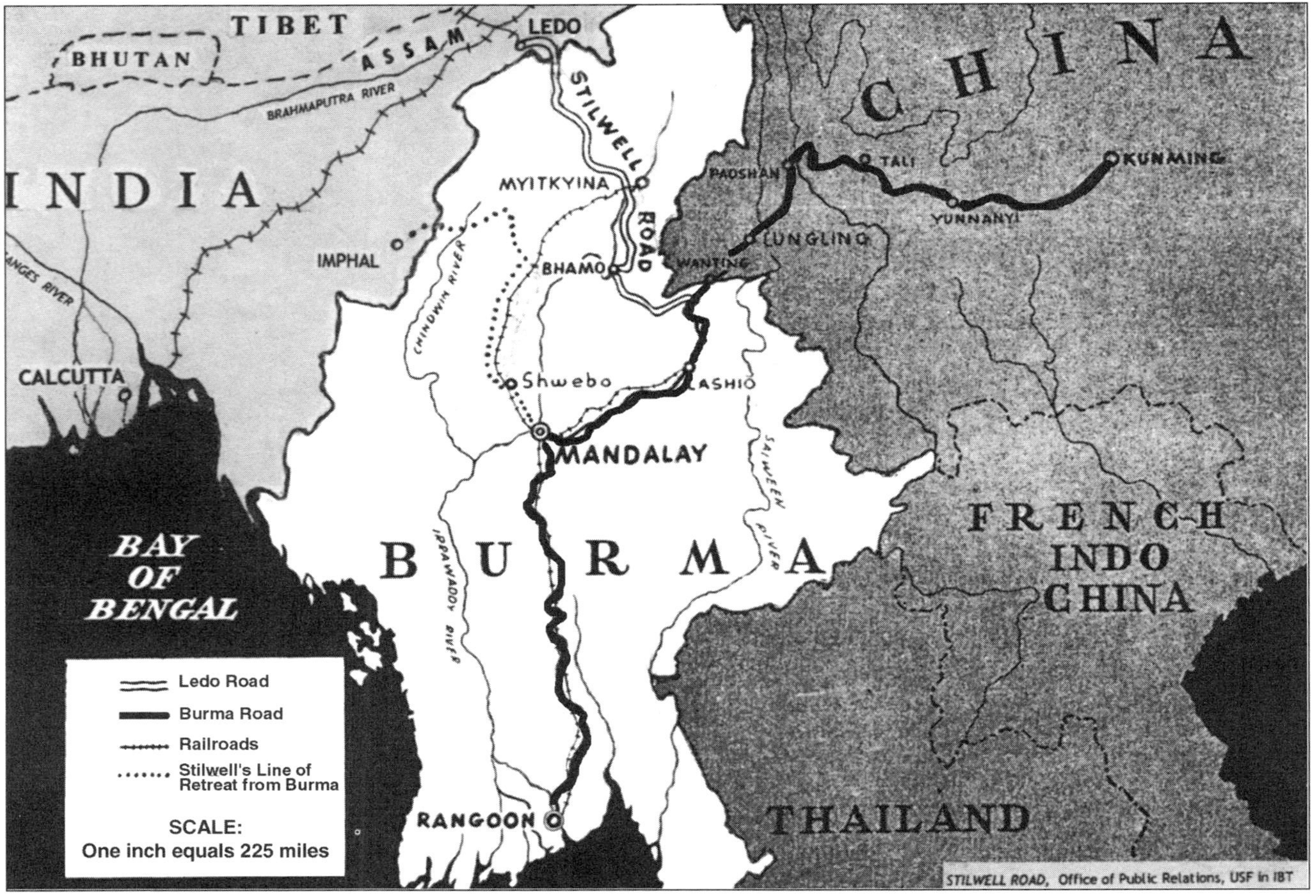

STILWELL ROAD, Office of Public Relations, USF in IBT

Legend:
- ═══ Ledo Road
- ━━━ Burma Road
- ┼┼┼ Railroads
- ••••• Stilwell's Line of Retreat from Burma

SCALE:
One inch equals 225 miles

Why the Road?

The Ledo Road and the war in Burma are among the least recognized undertakings of World War II. To appreciate the efforts involved in this theater it is necessary to provide insight into their background and strategic relevance. Following is an abbreviated synopsis of key events.

1931: The Japanese invade Manchuria and set up a puppet government. The Japanese military control the entire country.

1937: Japan launches a widescale offensive against China's entire Pacific Coast, and bombs the interior.

The Chinese anticipate the Japanese will soon close their Pacific Coast, thereby isolating China from the outside world. To provide access to China by its allies, construction is proposed of a road covering 430 miles in China and 170 in Burma. The road is to lead from Kunming in Yunnan Province, China to Lashio, Burma. From Lashio there is an existing rail line to Rangoon, Burma's capital and major port. The route for the road encompasses massive mountain ranges, precipitous valleys, desert, and dense forests. In 1935, in all of Yunnan province (the size of California), there were only 193 miles of surfaced roads. The Chinese had one small bulldozer, two air compressors, a limited supply of primitive hand tools, but hundreds of thousands of volunteer workers. Construction starts in October 1937.

Germany, Italy, and Japan sign mutual assistance agreements.

The Japanese, in an attempt to break the will of the Chinese people, sack Nanjing, slaughtering over 200,000 people.

1938: Japan seals China's entire Pacific Coast. In December the Burma Road opens to light traffic.

1940: In the fall the United States cuts off all exports of iron and steel to Japan.

1941: *February:* The United States extends Lend-Lease to China. Supplies are shipped to Rangoon and delivered by rail to Lashio, and then driven by truck over the Burma Road to Kunming.

August: President Franklin D. Roosevelt permits United States citizens to volunteer for service in China. General Claire Chennault organizes the Flying Tiger squadron there.

December 7: The Japanese bomb Pearl Harbor; the United States declares war on Germany and Japan.

1942: *March:* The Japanese invade Burma from Thailand, capture Rangoon, the rail line to Lashio, and close the Burma Road. General Stilwell is the Commander in Chief of all U.S. forces in China, Burma and India, and of the Chinese forces in Burma. These forces are badly defeated by the Japanese. They survive only by completing a heroic march through 300 miles of dense forest, and across rivers and high mountains. The departure point is the town of Shwebo, just north of Mandalay in central Burma. General Stilwell heads north to avoid the converging Japanese forces. With a few vehicles the General leads his party for 180 miles along a barely passable cart trail, roughly paralleling the Irrawaddy River, to the village of Mansi. There they abandon their few remaining jeeps and march west along narrow jungle trails for another 120 miles, reaching Imphal, India, 20 days after leaving Shwebo. Dr. Seagrave and his staff of Burmese nurses are part of the refugee column, and they provide invaluable medical assistance. The British forces are also defeated by the Japanese and are forced to withdraw back to India.

Late spring: The Japanese force their way eastward along the Burma Road into China to the Salween River. On the other side of the river, undermanned, underarmed, exhausted Chinese soldiers are all that stand between a formidable Japanese army and Kunming. But miraculously here the Japanese are stopped, and for the first time in Burma. To quote from Douglas Coe's *The Burma Road:*

Stilwell's Retreat: May 2–20, 1942

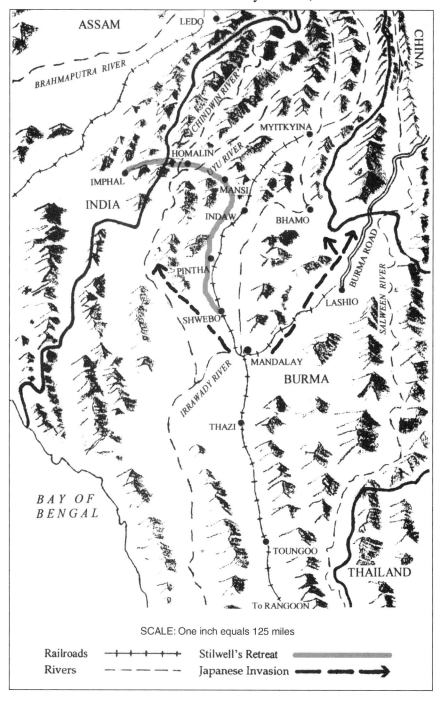

SCALE: One inch equals 125 miles

Railroads	Stilwell's Retreat
Rivers	Japanese Invasion

The Chinese occupied the near (right) bank and the Japanese the far (left) bank of the Salween Gorge. In the left center of this picture, the bridge over the Salween is barely discernible.

The Salween River Bridge. Early 1945, looking eastward toward the right bank. Both courtesy of U.S. Army Signal Corps.

…suddenly there was a new sound in the air…soon the whole gorge was filled with a roar that silenced even the Salween's waters. Around a bend came six P-40s of General Claire Chennault's Flying Tigers, moving in a tight formation that barely fit between the two steeply rising rock walls. The planes banked…and suddenly machine guns chattered. Booming explosions filled the air…from oil drums and munitions piles. The planes swept past…then dove for another run. The Japanese…began to scramble in terror up the sharp mountain at their back….Hastily [the Chinese]…were adding their own fire to the havoc caused by the planes. From that day on, every [Japanese] attempt to cross the river was stopped.

Summer: General Stilwell starts flying supplies, including large quantities of gasoline, over The Hump to China. The Chabua airbase, 40 miles northwest of Ledo, is the primary departure point. For the next two years this is one of the world's busiest airports, with cargo planes taking off loaded, or returning, every few minutes, day and night.

Fall: General Stilwell initiates construction of the Ledo Road. The road utilizes delivery by rail of supplies from the port of Calcutta to Ledo in the northeastern tip of India, then by truck convoy from there south, largely along existing jungle tracks, to the eastern portion of the Burma Road, and on to Kunming, China. This requires forcing the Japanese out of northern Burma. Only 15 miles of road are completed by the end of 1942.

Churchill and the British did not think it was possible to build the Ledo Road. That belief, and the later rapid U.S. success in capturing Pacific Islands, relegated the CBI to a lower military priority.

1943: *February:* Thirty-eight miles of road have been constructed, reaching the India-Burma border at the summit of Pangsau Pass (Elevation: 4,500 feet) in the rugged Patkai range.

March: Monsoon rains stop road construction until September.

October: The 38th and 22nd Chinese Infantry Divisions head south from Ledo to push the Japanese in northern Burma out of the path of the oncoming Ledo Road. These divisions were run out of Burma by the Japanese invasion in 1942. In India they had been reconstituted, trained, and reequipped by the Americans. They include a tank corps commanded by Colonel Rothwell Brown and manned by Chinese and U.S. soldiers.

At General Stilwell's urging, a highly qualified officer, Colonel Lewis A. Pick, assumes command of constructing the Ledo Road.

Lord Louis Mountbatten, Commander in Chief of the British forces in India and Burma, asks the U.S. to send a significant force to join General Orde Wingate's Chindits operating deep behind the Japanese lines in central Burma. President Franklin D. Roosevelt responds by calling for 3,000 volunteers for a "dangerous mission." Dubbed "Merrill's Marauders," they train as jungle fighters with the Chindits in India.

November: Road construction reaches mile 50. The village of Shingbwiyang (mile 103) is captured from the Japanese. Construction of an airport there begins.

December: Road construction reaches Shingbwiyang.

1944: *February:* Stillwell transfers Merrill's Marauders to his command. They walk south along the old track from Ledo, then circle through the jungle to the rear of the Japanese front-line positions. This cuts the Japanese supply and communication lines and puts them in a vise between the Marauders and Stilwell's Chinese forces, causing their retreat. All of the Marauders' supplies had to be air dropped to them.

March: Stilwell's Chinese forces attack the Japanese at Maingkwan (approximately mile 143), and the Marauders attack their rear defenses at Walawbum (approximately mile 153). After a sharp battle the Japanese withdraw. A week later, using similar tactics, the Japanese are defeated in a fierce battle at Jambu Bum Pass, the gateway to the Mogaung Valley (mile 178).

Some 115,000 Japanese troops and support personnel, carrying only three weeks of rations, invade India from Burma, intent on capturing the East Indian towns of Imphal and Kohima. If successful, they would trap the Allied forces in Assam and northern Burma, and cut off all supplies to China. The British and Indian forces, outnumbered by as much as seven-to-one, fight desperately to buy time. In just 11 days the 12,000-man Indian Fifth Division is airlifted from the Arakan front in Burma to Imphal. Additional reinforcements and supplies pour in. As the defenders gain strength, the Japanese, exhorted by their commander "to expect...almost annihilation," suffer appalling losses from battle, disease, and starvation.

April: The Ledo Road construction reaches Warazup (mile 189); Japanese outposts had been driven back from both Shaduzup and Warazup.

March 1944: A column of Marauders with pack mules crosses a tributary of the Chindwin River, one of the main waterways in northern Burma. Photograph by Sergeant David B. Richardson; courtesy of the Merrill's Marauders Association.

March 1944: Marauders pass bodies of Japanese soldiers who were killed shortly before, while attempting an ambush of the preceding patrol. Photograph by Sergeant David B. Richardson; courtesy of the Merrill's Marauders Association.

Taking a disabled Marauder to a jungle landing strip for evacuation. The nine-mile mountain trail by mule or stretcher was too hazardous, so the Marauders made a raft and poled the soldier down the river behind enemy lines. Photograph by Bernard Hoffman; courtesy of the Merrill's Marauders Association.

April 1944: Has'tnshingyang, Burma: an L-1A evacuation plane approaches an improvised runway for landing. Rice paddy dikes have been leveled in the runway area. Each incapacitated Marauder was evacuated in such a plane, able to carry only a stretcher, the soldier, and the pilot. Photograph by Lieutenant Lubin; courtesy of the Merrill's Marauders Association.

May: The Marauders and Chinese infantry occupy and put into operation the undamaged airport, nearby, at Myitkyina (mile 268; pronounced "Mitch-in-awe"). This is the only all-weather airport in northern Burma. The Japanese refuel planes there for harassing Allied Hump flights. The 5,000 Japanese fortify their positions in the city, the key to controlling northern Burma, and dig in for a long siege. The battle is brutal. American engineers and men from service units are given rifles and thrown into the fox holes. Many have had little combat training.

Chinese forces cross the Salween River, pushing the Japanese west toward Tengchung.

July: Chinese forces reach Tengchung, where the Japanese have dug in. On July 8, four months after their invasion, the Japanese withdraw from Kohima and Imphal, having lost 65,000 men. This battle was the largest and most pivotal in the India-Burma Campaign. From this point on, Japanese power in Burma declines.

August: In the first week, Stilwell's forces at Myitkyina take the city after a 75-day siege. The few remaining Japanese escape down the river.

September: Tengchung falls. Stilwell's forces reach Bhamo (mile 372). The Japanese at Bhamo are besieged and the balance of Stilwell's forces continue east toward Wanting at the Burma-China border.

November: The Chinese take Lungling after a six-month siege.

December: Bhamo falls after a siege of three months.

1945: *January:* Namkham falls to Stilwell's forces (mile 439). Wanting falls to the Chinese (mile 507), removing the last Japanese resistance on the road between Ledo and Kunming.

February: The first convoy from Ledo reaches Kunming.

May: The British defeat the Japanese at Lashio, Mandalay, and Rangoon, removing their presence from Burma.

The campaign in Burma was summarized in an article by *YANK* staff correspondent Sergeant David B. Richardson, published after completion of the first convoy to Kunming:

> In the battle for Northern Burma, Merrill's Marauders and their successor, the Mars Task Force, were the catalyst for success. Walking along jungle trails, fording rivers, and crossing mountains, they

repeatedly sneaked around the flanks and cut in to throw up road-blocks in the rear of the Japs, causing their collapse up front for lack of supplies. These maneuvers were coordinated with the American trained and armed Chinese 22nd and 38th divisions and their tank corps which moved south down the Ledo Road and acted as the hammer against the Marauder anvil in crushing Japanese resistance.

But these forces alone could never have accomplished what they did. They needed the Tenth Air Force, whose Troop Carrier and Combat Cargo planes were the main supply line for the fighting troops with daily air drops of tons of food and ammunition and equipment, and whose fighters and bombers knocked out hundreds of bridges and other objectives in the path of the advance, bedsides reducing the Jap airforce in Burma to the point where the sight of a single Jap plane was a rarity. They needed the American-led (OSS-101) Kachin rangers, whose behind-the-lines guerilla activity chased the Japs out of the mountains. The rangers also rescued over 400 Allied airmen downed in the unrelenting Burma jungle. They needed all these combat outfits, plus the thousands of GIs behind the lines in Engineer and Quartermaster and Signal Corps and hospital outfits who serviced them.

And they needed the British and Indians of Wingate's Chindits, who were landed by Colonel Phil Cochran's First Air Commando gliders 150 miles behind Jap lines to spend months raiding Jap bases, wreck-ing railway tracks, blocking roads and blowing bridges. And the British 36th Division, which drove down the right flank of the main Chinese offensive toward Mandalay, forcing the Japs to split their defenses.

The Chinese Expeditionary Force launched its campaign by crossing the Salween River in May of 1944 and drove through to the [Burma] road junction from China. This Force did the ground fighting on that side of the campaign, mostly thousands of feet high in the Kaoli Kung mountains known as "The Hump," but they also needed support. They got it from the American Y-Force Operations Staff of Brig. Gen. Frank Dorn, which provided them with radio communi-cations, tactical assistance and supply lines. And they got it from the Fourteenth Air Force, which did the same job of supply and close air support in China that the Tenth did in Burma, only against the greater odds of a stronger Jap air force and a gasoline shortage there.

What made the campaign so tough was not just the tenacious enemy, but the harsh climate and terrain. The June to September monsoons — worst in the world — bogged down trucks in hub-high muck, kept planes grounded or caused hundreds of them to crash in violent storms, and shot up the disease rate. There were mountains rising to 5,000 and 7,000 feet, and jungles as thick as those in New Guinea, and thousands of rivers and streams. In the winter there was bitter cold, when infantrymen couldn't carry more than one blanket, and in the summer intense heat and rains — 140 inches in most places.

It was the walkingest campaign of the century, because it was fought in places where there were few roads. The Marauders and Chindits hoofed it for some 600 miles, and the Chinese 38th and the Mars Task Force did almost as much. Unlike the infantry in most campaigns of the war, the Chinese and GIs and British here had to carry their own packs all the way instead of slinging them on trucks. They carried all of their own arms, ammunition, food, water, and personal equipment. Mules carried the pack howitzers, radios, and medical supplies.

As far as GIs were concerned, it was a makeshift campaign in which bulldozer operators became tank drivers, clerks and radiomen became mule skinners, engineers became infantrymen, ordnance mechanics became tank gunners, and muleskinners became artillerymen. And it was a campaign where there was nothing in a town when it was captured — only a few thatched huts and a lot of dead Japs.

Sergeant David B. Richardson, YANK *correspondent, who accompanied the Marauders on much of their harrowing campaign.* Courtesy of David B. Richardson.

Heading south on Pangsau Pass, October 1944. We had to be towed through the mud.
Courtesy of Edward Gariepy.

The Ledo Road winding north through the Pangsau Pass, just south of Ledo. Elevation: 4,500 feet.
Courtesy of U.S. Army Signal Corps.

WORLD WAR II SYNOPSIS:
1945

1945, January – August
January: U.S.S.R. forces capture Warsaw.
February: U.S. forces capture Manila.
March: U.S. forces capture Iwo Jima.
April: Okinawa Island is invaded.
     Mussolini is executed.
     U.S.S.R. forces reach Berlin; Hitler commits suicide.
     German troops in Italy surrender.
May: U.S.S.R. forces liberate Vienna.
     Germany surrenders.
     Rangoon falls to the British forces; the Japanese are forced out of Burma.
June: U.S. forces capture Okinawa.
August: Hiroshima and Nagasaki are destroyed by Atom bombs dropped by the U.S.
     Japan surrenders.

Taming a Mighty Land

On October 12, 1944 Company A moved out of Ledo over the rugged Pangsau Pass, down the road past Shingbwiyang and Tingkawk-Sakan to mile point 170, and set up camp there. The battalion had been assigned the 25-mile stretch of road from Tingkawk-Sakan to Warazup. In building the road, the first phase was to open a trace that combat troops could use in dry weather and for supplying them. The second phase was to widen the road, and install necessary bridges, culverts and gravel so heavy two-way traffic could travel on it in both wet and dry weather. When we arrived it was a 20-foot-wide dirt road with many river fords. When we left it was straighter, 33-feet wide, heavily graveled, and with many new bridges and culverts. In straightening one two-mile section of the road, Company A moved 26,260 yards of dirt.

We were very impressed when we found that a pipeline had been laid from Ledo south along the road. This was vital in fueling our trucks and construction equipment. The pipeline required careful surveillance, which meant patrolling it by foot through the jungle. This was needed since the natives found they could loosen the flanges so the joints would leak, enabling them to collect valuable fuel. The pipeline engineers did not object to losing the small amount of fuel. Their concern was that such leaks could catch fire and damage the line, cutting off deliveries.

Winter weather in northern Burma was superb: clear, cloudless days, low humidity, temperatures in the 70's during the days, and mild at

The Ledo Road
Ledo (Mile 0) to Mong-Yu (Mile 478)

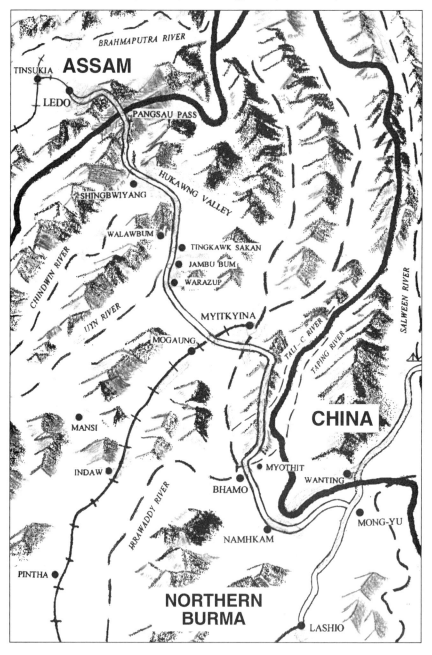

Company A's camp in northern Burma. Courtesy of 1875th Battalion.

night. We lived in large, pyramidal tents. Our camp was located on a shelf above a clear river, ideal for fishing and swimming — and for bridging. Building that bridge was my platoon's assignment. Large timbers were cut from the forest and driven as pilings into the river with a diesel-power shovel. More timbers were cut for the joists, decking, curbs and cross-braces. It was a sturdy structure.

The approach to the bridge was down a steep slope. The road curved sharply to the left onto the bridge; a hill on the left blocked any view of the bridge or of our construction site just before the bridge. Frequently, GI trucks came around that curve at high speeds. When the drivers saw our construction crew, machinery, or supplies, they had to slam on their brakes to avoid a collision. Hoping to prevent such accidents, we installed signs along the approach warning drivers of the dangerous curve and setting progressively lower speed limits.

Not long after we installed the signs, a driver came barreling down the slope in a truck with no roof on the cab. He paid no attention to the signs and had to slam on his brakes to avoid hitting a parked truck that was partially blocking the road. I ordered the truck driver to pull to the side of the road, told him to stay there until he was authorized to

The swimming dock. Courtesy of 1875th Battalion.

The bridge downstream from our camp. The swimming dock can be seen under the bridge.

proceed, and stationed a platoon corporal as a guard to see that the driver obeyed. After directing the corporal to do whatever was necessary to keep the truck from moving, I headed back around the hill to the river's edge, where most of our construction activity was taking place.

Several minutes later, I heard a gunshot. I raced back to the bend in the road and then slowed to a saunter just before coming in sight of the truck. My first glance was one of pure relief: the driver was alive, although he was sitting rigidly in his truck and his face was the color of new-fallen Arctic snow. The corporal had his rifle pointed at the driver's heart. I ambled up to the corporal and asked him what had happened. He explained that the driver had been cussing me out, so he had decided to put a stop to it. I told the corporal to keep up the good work, and then returned to our construction site. After about a half-hour, I went back to the driver and told him to tell his commanding officer and all his fellow drivers that each subsequent speeder would be pulled over for double the time of the most recent speeder. Apparently, word got around; we had no further such incidents.

During this period many combat units passed along the road by our camp, both American and Chinese. They were walking: the Americans with long easy strides; the Chinese with short rapid strides. The Americans started out heavily laden with equipment and supplies,

Chinese infantry fording a stream on the Ledo Road, moving to the front line.
Courtesy of U.S. Army Signal Corps.

GI's in jeeps, passing a unit of Chinese troops heading to the front lines.

Hacking through the Burmese jungle.
Courtesy of U.S. Army Signal Corps.

Courtesy of *YANK* magazine.

The python and Lieutenant King.

the Chinese with very little. As miles passed, the Americans cast items off until they were down to the basic necessities. The Chinese picked up these cast-offs, happily carrying their new burden.

We also worked on straightening the road. This involved hacking our way through the jungle and bamboo underbrush to survey a line. Then we brought in bulldozers to clear the roadway. During this work we frequently saw wildlife. One type was a three-foot long lizard with an 18-inch-long tail, tapering rapidly to a point. They were harmless, but very fast and hard to catch. One of my men saw such a lizard's tail in the underbrush while clearing trace and grabbed hold of it. Much to his surprise, it wasn't a lizard but a huge python. When the snake stuck its head out from the underbrush, the soldier screamed for help and his buddy smashed the beast's head with a brush hook. The python was taken back to camp, and was found to weigh 125 pounds; it was 17 feet long and 9 inches in diameter. The soldier skinned the python and kept the skin, and the local natives, for whom the python was a delicacy, had a memorable feast.

The python is stretched out back at camp. It is 17 feet long!

A week's supply of venison for the company.

Game was numerous. All four companies had very tasty venison several times a week. Tigers were seen occasionally; a few were shot and their skins kept for trophies. I saw one black leopard. There were huge squirrels, and many large monkeys who loved to swing through the treetops emitting loud whooping calls. There were also scorpions, tarantulas, three-inch long leeches, and clouds of mosquitoes. The scorpions and tarantulas would climb into our boots at night. In the mornings we faithfully turned our boots upside down and shook them hard. Any unwelcome visitor that fell out was dispatched with a quick blow from the boot heel.

The leeches were the most prevalent problem. They would cling to foliage and fall or brush off onto passersby, often unnoticed. They quickly locked their mouths onto any bare skin and gorged themselves on the victim's blood. Sometimes they could be induced to fall off by burning them with a cigarette lighter. Otherwise they were cut off, but this required an early visit to a medic to ensure that the head had been completely removed from the victim. On one occasion a fuzzy caterpillar fell off a bush, curled into a ball, and rolled down my bare arm. I thought nothing of it — initially. But it had hundreds of tiny quills which became embedded in my skin, itched brutally, and caused a raw, festering, month-long sore covering my left arm from elbow to wrist.

For recreation, besides hunting and basketball, we had movies several times a week at an improvised battalion theater. When the movies were being shown, the beam of light swarmed with millions of

GI hunters shot and skinned these two tigers, and sent their pelts home.

mosquitoes. The bitter Atabrine pill was our savior. On another occasion, a first-class USO troupe even came to perform; the Troupe featured Hollywood stars Pat O'Brien and Jinx Falkenburg.

Unfortunately, during our work at this section of the Ledo Road, the battalion lost three men. One died of a tumor, which had nothing to do with Burma or the war; one was hit by falling debris from blasting while clearing the right of way; and one died from cerebral malaria.

On November 28, 1944 the battalion received orders to move south along the road trace through Myitkyina and 90 miles further to a point approximately 15 miles north of Bhamo, where the Japanese were still under siege. My platoon was designated as the lead element. We carried our small arms, had ample ammunition, and were assigned the battalion half-track, an armored truck with wheels in the front and steel tracks in the rear instead of wheels. It was equipped with a 50-caliber machine gun on a swivel mount. We followed an unimproved dirt road south of Mogaung, then drove up over a range of high, steep hills. At the crest the roads were soaked from recent rains and were covered with slick clay. The road-bed sloped down away from the uphill side. In India and Burma all traffic followed the English practice of driving on the left. But when driving in these conditions around blind right-hand curves, we did not dare drive on the outside for fear of skidding off the road and down the mountainside. So we went around those curves hugging the uphill side as closely as possible and honking our horns. Fortunately we met no oncoming traffic and arrived safely in Myitkyina. There we crossed the wide Irrawaddy River by ferry and camped for the night on the far side.

A half-track, but without the armor over the cab and gun platform, and without the 50-caliber machine gun.

The Ledo Road, cutting through the Kumon Mountains, just north of Mogaung and Myitkyina. Courtesy of U.S. Army Signal Corps.

Above left: Ferrying across the Irrawaddy. Above right: A close-up of the two-lane bridge across the mighty Irrawaddy River. Below: These bridges were constructed after our trip. The one-lane bridge on the right was first constructed, followed by the two-lane bridge on the left.

Bridge photographs courtesy of the U.S. Army Signal Corps.

Before we headed toward Bhamo, I had been given an aerial photograph of the area to which we had been assigned and knew the approximate mileage we had to traverse. The next morning we followed the trail south. The trail consisted of two wheel-tracks through the grass. It led along the east side of the Irrawaddy River Valley, then climbed high into the hills and generally followed the ridge lines. We met no traffic during the trip.

Company A's assigned portion of the road lay between two rivers, several miles apart, and was discernable on my aerial photograph. The nearer river was immediately preceded by a very steep descent to it. After crossing this river, there was a relatively level valley leading to the second river. We made the descent, forded the river, and pulled off into a grove of tall trees across the road from Kadaw. We rested there; some of the men wandered around, and I checked the vehicles and my photograph.

We continued on along the trace for a mile or two and came to a small, tree-covered, round hill, right in the middle of the valley and completely blocking the road which led around it. I stopped the convoy, climbed the hill, and saw the road leading straight ahead for about one-half mile, then curving into a thick woods: a perfect point for a Japanese sniper. I had the platoon position themselves on the hill, and got in my command car with the half-track following behind, buttoned up and ready to fire. One of my corporals was driving the car, the windshield was down, and I had a fully loaded M-1 rifle at the ready. We proceeded slowly down the road. If there was a lone sniper there, he could get in one shot with his bolt-action rifle. Before he could fire a second shot, my M-1 semi-automatic could fire all six of its rounds, and the 50-caliber machine gun could blow the whole tree away. We might have a casualty, but the sniper would be obliterated. I was more concerned about a Japanese patrol being in ambush on the left side of the road where the ground sloped up and provided ample cover. We came to the woods and the bend in the road without incident. As we passed the tree with the vantage point looking straight back along the road, I looked up. There was the sniper's platform, some 15 feet above ground, and pointing straight down the road; it was empty.

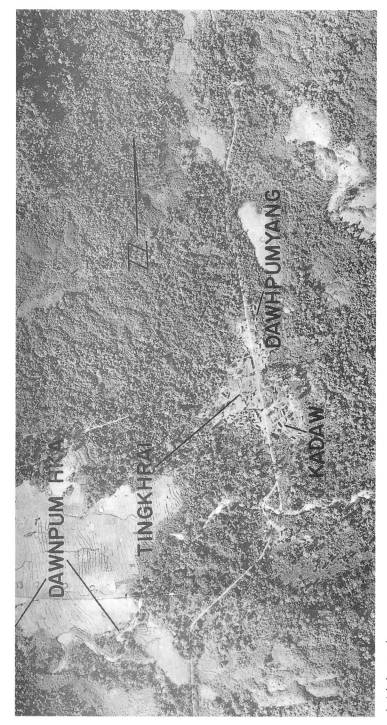

Aerial photograph.

Our trail south, into the jungle.

My command car and trailer.

We regrouped, and continued down the road with the car and half-track in the lead until we reached the second river. On the near right bank were the remains of a Japanese camp, complete with trenches and foxholes. We could hear the sound of heavy artillery firing in Bhamo some 15 miles to the south. Our camp had to have water, and I had not seen a suitable campsite at the first river so the platoon was put to work cleaning up the Japanese campsite in the few daylight hours left. I was not happy with the choice, but had not seen a better location. After a few minutes of work, one of my sergeants approached and said that he had wandered around the site at the first river where we had rested and thought it was much better. I told the rest of the platoon to stop working and rest, and jumped into a jeep with the sergeant. He was right: that was a far more attractive site, with water, tree cover from the sun, relatively flat land, and little undergrowth. I recalled the platoon.

We had a small D-4 bulldozer with us. Early the next morning we put it to work clearing the site. It ran from dawn to dusk for several days until the fuel ran out. Areas had been cleared and locations marked out for the headquarters tent, mess tent, orderly and supply tents, personnel tents, showers, washbasins, and latrines. The rest of the company arrived two days later. The company remained at this location until the battalion left for home months later. Ours was the only company that did not move to a more attractive site during our stay in this area, but our facilities were continually improved.

The rest of the battalion followed and took up contiguous stretches of the road south of Company A. From the battalion history:

All the companies bent to the tasks of widening the trail into a road, improving grades, blind curves and mud holes that were really swamps. Thousands of feet of culvert were installed.

"A" Company installed three Bailey Bridges, 170ft. and two 70fts. All in all, we had moved several thousand yards of earth, straightened and widened dozens of curves, and drained it all.

Traffic, when we first arrived, was a mere handful of vehicles. Occasionally a lone truck would pass. Then the road became passable — temporary bridges and fords had been built.... A Chinese armored division passed through on its way to Bhamo. Bhamo fell. Chinese and Indian troops, pontoons, bridges, food and other supplies moved on to the fighting forces besieging Namkham....

The scenic views through the hills, just north of Kadaw.

Sergeant Kanter with a primed block of TNT. This is the primer for removing a large tree from the path of the Ledo Road, using one-half of a box of TNT.

Cutting and filling the Ledo Road.

Grading the road.

Gravelling the road.

The finished product. All four photographs courtesy of 1875th Battalion.

The 170-foot Bailey Bridge.
Courtesy of U.S. Army Signal Corps.

One of the 70-foot Bailey Bridges.
Courtesy of U.S. Army Signal Corps.

A destroyed Japanese tank.

Bhamo in ruins. Both photos courtesy of U.S. Army Signal Corps.

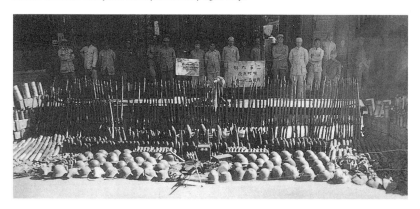

Japanese arms captured after the seige of Bhamo.

At Christmas time we hosted units of the Mars Task Force, the successor to Merrill's Marauders which had played such a key role in the fighting in North Burma and at Myitkyina. Merrill's Marauders had experienced such high losses from combat, disease and exhaustion that the remnants of the unit had been withdrawn and the unit had been reconstituted. The Mars Task Force was marching on to the front.

The Marauders cross a stream behind enemy lines.
Photo courtesy of *YANK's* Magic Carpet.

"A" Company, in January, continued their work on the stretch of road that really needed speed control. They hauled 3,500 cubic yards of gravel to their road and moved some 4,000 cubic yards of dirt to eliminate the tortuous hairpin turns in their area.

I well remember the first convoy to traverse the road. It was a long-awaited event, and one which had required an enormous effort, both in combat and construction. We had been under great pressure to have the road ready as soon as the Japanese were driven out of northern and central Burma. The winter weather was superb, clear, dry, and cool.

The following paragraph is a condensation of a more detailed account of this event published in Douglas Coe's book, *The Burma Road*:

On January 12, 1945 the first convoy of trucks, loaded with supplies and munitions for China left Ledo on their historic trip. The convoy was led by General Pick, Road Commander. It traveled to Myitkyina and laid over there for seven days, waiting for the final Japanese resistance to be eliminated southeast of Bhamo. There a Chinese driver joined each American driver in the vehicles' cabs. Eleven days

The lead truck; first convoy from Ledo to Kunming.

The first convoy reaches Ledo–Burma Road Junction. Both photos courtesy of U.S. Army Signal Corps.

Crossing the border at Wanting, China.

The officials led by General Pick, passing in review at Kunming.
Both photos courtesy of U.S. Army Signal Corps.

after leaving Ledo the convoy pulled into Bhamo with 113 vehicles. There they waited two days for Namkham to be taken, eliminating the last Japanese resistance, and took another two days to reach that village. The next day, at the junction with the old road, they linked up with the Chinese force that had driven the Japanese west from the Salween River gorge. On January 28th the convoy reached Wanting, China. On February 5th, the 24th day after leaving Ledo, the convoy entered Kunming. The vehicles had flags waving and the drivers were in dress uniforms, complete with ties. This was the first of many convoys over the coming months.

When the convoy came along the high ridges that were a part of Company A's assigned section, General Pick stopped it, got out of his command car, and approached one of our enlisted men who was operating a road grader. The General had noticed that the road had been built on the crest of the ridges flanking the floor of the Irrawaddy River Valley far below. He asked the grader operator, a Corporal named

Chinese troops celebrating after the victory at Namkham. Courtesy of U.S. Army Signal Corps.

A convoy kicking up dust on the Ledo Road.

Maloney, why the road had been built on the ridges instead of in the valley — which obviously would have been much easier. The operator's answer was classic, "Don't ask me General, I just work here." Many of us had asked the same question, but had never received a credible answer.

Being a convoy driver was difficult and dangerous. In the dry, winter weather, the vehicles would kick up huge clouds of dust that obscured vision and covered the windshields. To see the truck ahead — which was essential to avoid collisions — a driver had two choices. He could tailgate the vehicle ahead, risking a collision if that truck slowed or stopped suddenly. Or he could lag far behind where the dust thinned out, greatly stretching the convoy. The latter action had the added problem that dust on the windshield blinded a driver when driving from bright sunlight into deep jungle shade. Sunlight reflecting off the dusty windshield prevented the driver from seeing anything in the dark shadows ahead. In addition, the gravel road developed corduroy-like bumps with heavy travel. On curves, these had the same effect as ice — greatly reducing friction. At significant speeds this could cause a vehicle to spin and go over the side of the road. In mountainous country this often resulted in the loss of driver, truck, and contents. Drivers wanted open cabs so they would have a chance to jump clear if the truck left the road.

The driver of this truck forgot to downshift into low gear, coming down a steep grade.
Courtesy of U.S. Army Signal Corps.

In the rainy season the roads got muddy, causing similar problems with spattered windshields and slick roads. Inexperienced drivers frequently tried to keep a truck's speed under control going down steep mountain slopes by using only the brakes. This would cause the brake lining to overheat and catch fire, incinerating the entire vehicle. Fortunately the drivers did not have to drive the empty trucks back to Ledo. The trucks were left in China for the use of Chiang Kai-shek's army and the drivers flew back over The Hump to Ledo, shortly to join another convoy.

In February a large Bailey suspension bridge over the Taping River near Myothit, our H&S Company's site, was opened. Several weeks later H&S Company undertook to improve the foundation for the upstream anchor on the west end of the bridge. This involved some excavation between the anchor and the bridge. During this work, a large rig, including a ten-ton truck with a small bulldozer in the truck and pulling a heavily loaded trailer, entered the bridge. The heavy load caused the anchor to slip forward. The cable-tower tilted toward the bridge, dropping the upstream side of the bridge decking several feet so it sloped steeply down toward the water. This made the bridge impassable. Word rapidly reached headquarters in Ledo and within an hour or two the top brass flew over the site to evaluate the damage. Helped by

The suspension bridge over the Taping River. Courtesy of 1875th Battalion.

low water during the dry season, H&S Company used bulldozers to haul convoy trucks across the river until a pontoon bridge was installed. This served the convoys until the suspension bridge was fully repaired.

Maintaining the Road

We continued to improve the Ledo Road. By late winter road construction had largely been completed and we spent our time maintaining it. This required fewer man-hours. Rather than have the men go out on the job every day and just stand around for part of it, I requested that the company commander approve a program for giving the men in each of the four platoons one day a week off for personal use, from Monday through Friday. This was done. The amount of fresh venison increased. The soldiers obtained chickens from natives and started raising their own. We had fresh eggs for breakfast. Throughout the battalion, basketball courts and softball fields proliferated.

Our GIs became more resourceful in gathering local food. The nearby Tali-C River was relatively large, with clear, fast-flowing water teeming with fish. It is difficult to feed a fish dinner to 180 men when relying on fishing rods; however, two or three one-quarter pound blocks of TNT exploded in the river proved adequate for the task. Other ventures were not so successful. Golden Cocks were plentiful here. They resembled pheasants, but were about 50 percent bigger and had gorgeous multi-colored plumage. One was caught, cooked to perfection and served. I was given a large, moist drumstick. It had a marvelous aroma. I bit into it and nothing happened. I cut off a small piece of meat with a sharp knife. The meat was as tough as the sole of my army boot. Golden Cocks were scrubbed from our menu. Another culinary venture involved obtaining a young water buffalo. The hindquarters were roasted and basted on a newly-cut bamboo spit for three days. The aroma was delightful, but the meat had a bitter taste. We later learned the taste came from the *green* bamboo spit we used.

Being mindful of the coming monsoon season I developed a plan for installing wood floors under the enlisted men's tents. In our area there were some abandoned two-story frame houses in a deserted village. I located the former village chief and asked if we could trade for the floors in the houses. We would leave the houses standing. He agreed. We collected a lot of goodies received from home, especially bars of soap.

Company A basketball game: March 11, 1945.

The day's catch!

The hindquarters of the young water buffalo, prior to cooking.

Thanksgiving, we think (hope). Courtesy of 1875th Battalion.

One of the native houses that donated its wooden floors for our camp.
Courtesy of U.S. Army Signal Corps.

We could have been court-martialed if we had used any army-issued supplies for trading. For a basketful of supplies, we got the floors. We put temporary supports under the floors and with power saws cut the flooring and joists around the floor's periphery. A slit was cut in one side of the house the height and breadth of the floor and the floor was pulled out through it. The floors were a big improvement during the monsoon.

From my letter of March 5, 1945:

> Yesterday there wasn't much cooking so I decided in a flash to try to drive into China. Just then four of my non-commissioned officers came along so the five of us grabbed our rifles, canteens, cameras and a shovel and axe. About ten miles north of here there is an ancient cart trail that leads eastward up into the hills and to the China border — which at that point is a river. The trail was barely wide enough for a jeep. We twisted and turned, forded streams and climbed up around the side of a mountain. At one place the road was partially washed out but we thought we could make it so I put the jeep in low-low gear and started across. The jeep was half way across when it slipped sideways in the mud, right towards a river about 100 feet below. However there was a stump there and all was OK, except that the jeep was bellied up on a rock at a 45 degree angle. We dug, wheezed, and shoved and finally got it off the rock and back up to the road.
>
> We proceeded along, filling in ditches here and cutting trees and logs there. At one spot we came to an old suspension bridge leading off to one side of the road. It had four 1¼-inch cables stretched

The rock gorge and suspension bridge.

A view of the gorge downstream from the suspension bridge.

across a rock gorge and a wooden roadway. It had probably carried foot travelers and ox carts, I doubt that a vehicle had ever crossed it. We didn't, for the simple reason that the far end of the bridge had either been blown out or fell out. The rock gorge was a beautiful sight — from 50 to 80 feet deep and in places only about 30 feet wide. It was lined on either side with towering, weather-beaten slabs of granite. The water was alternately a brilliant placid blue and a churning rushing foam. In one of the pools we saw three otter swimming along, but there was no possible way to get to them if we did shoot them, so we didn't.

We continued on the road as far as we could, and then got out and started to hike. We walked about three miles and came out on the rocky bank of our river. At that point the river was wide, moderately swift and sparkling clear. It seemed as though we were in the

The explorers in China, sans clothing.

middle of eternity — the calm stillness of the jungle pervaded, yet always that semi-audible undertone of birds, insects and the bubbling sunlit water. It was really gorgeous.

At the water's edge we saw small objects glistening like gold in the sunlight. We scooped them up with great excitement. They were gold nuggets! But having had a superb high-school chemistry teacher, I recalled his admonition: "Fools gold, lead sulfide, is crystalline and readily fractures upon impact. Gold is amorphous and doesn't." Our gold nuggets were crystalline and did fracture.

On the other side of the river was China. So off came our clothes and across we went — brrr but it was frigid. Some pictures were taken of us in China, sans clothing. We recrossed the river and dressed. On the return trip we were a bit more careful, exercised our pick and axe a bit more and had no trouble. At present the trail is used by Kachins and Chinese as a pack route. We passed two or three small burro trains laden with wares and saki [fermented rice wine]. They carry the saki in sections of huge bamboo stalks.

Above: Kachin tribespeople. Right: The "headless tribesmen" are simply the result of an inexperienced photographer, but the image clearly shows the razor sharp sword to advantage.

During the period when the men had a day a week off, an incident occurred that might well have had an unfortunate outcome. On a day off, one of my men, a fine young, tall, well-built but naïve farmhand from the midwest, took a stroll out of our camp along one of the native trails leading into the forest. Along the way he met a young Kachin woman and apparently made an unwelcomed approach toward her. She screamed, her male companions came running down the trail, and one man drew his sword. The Kachin men always carried razor sharp swords for protection. One Kachin slashed at the soldier, who put up his left hand to ward off the blow; he was severely cut across the palm. He rushed back to our first-aid room where his hand was bandaged to stop the bleeding. I was in camp and was called to the first-aid hut. I took one look at the hand, confirmed the severity of the cut and told the soldier to grab any necessary belongings for a trip to the hospital and jump into my jeep. I went to the company commander, explained the situation and asked that the man be put on temporary duty at the hospital until the wound was completely healed. It was certain that the natives would soon be wandering through the camp looking for the soldier. We could only hope that the incident had happened so fast that they would only recognize him by the bandage on his hand. It was unthinkable to let the soldier get into trouble over this incident. The company commander agreed. We took off and drove the 107 miles to Myitkyina, rather than the 15 miles to Bhamo. Both had hospitals, but Myitkyina was safer. The Kachins wandered daily through our camp for weeks glancing at the men's hands, and finally gave up. The soldier returned to camp, his scar was barely discernable, and we kept him inconspicuous.

On February 24, 1945 I was relieved of assignment as a platoon leader in Company A and was assigned to battalion headquarters as Assistant S-3 Officer. The S-3 Section is a staff function reporting directly to the battalion commander. It is the plans and operations department and oversees all of the battalion engineering activities. The S-3 Officer was Major Stevenson. Before the war he had held an important position with the Texas Highway Commission; he was a very able civil engineer and a fine person. We got along very well. The Major stayed close to headquarters so I did most of the S-3 fieldwork. This gave me a chance to get more familiar with all the battalion's construction activities and to use my engineering background more effectively.

But for almost two years I had trained and led the first platoon of Company A, and at the time of my transfer I was the only original officer left in the company. In a letter to my parents, I wrote:

Left: Major Stevenson and Lieutenant King. Right: Major Stevenson in the battalion operations office, Myothit, Burma. Courtesy of 1875th Battalion.

First platoon, Company A, Kadaw, central Burma.

I am really fond of the men in Company A and especially of my platoon. Although some of the men are almost old enough to be my dad, I feel like a father to them. I know what they can and can't do, their moods and temperaments, their likes and dislikes, their family life. We get along perfectly — they always treat me with courtesy and respect, even though I kid them and often get down and dig in the ditch beside them. As far as I am concerned it is the best platoon in the army (they have the best record in the battalion) and it will break my heart to leave them.

Shortly after my transfer to Assistant S-3 I fell heir to the additional job of Liaison Officer between our battalion and a Chinese labor battalion. They were helping us straighten, widen, and gravel the Ledo Road. As Liaison Officer my job was to coordinate their work with that of the 1875th, and to meet with their officers once or twice a week to review our joint operations. I developed a distaste for the officers of Chiang Kai-shek's army. To me they were arrogant, lazy, and incompetent. The Chinese soldiers were the opposite. Most were village peasants, pressed into service at the point of a bayonet. They were industrious, bright, and had initiative. I could outline a project for them to do, go away, and return to find it finished and done exceedingly well.

There was a perk to my assignment of working with the Chinese, as I wrote in a letter on May 13 to my parents:

Nothing like a little culture, even in Burma, so the other night I went to the opera. Yep, an honest to goodness opera. The Chinese unit stationed near here had what is their equivalent of our USO visit them and put on a series of operas, one of which I went to see. They were very good hosts, giving me a comfortable deck chair right in front of the stage, an interpreter to tell me what was going on, and a synopsis of the plot typewritten in English. It was a treat. The stage was made out of bamboo, was quite large, and nicely decorated. The orchestra consisted of a bunch of tin pans on which the musicians beat and raised an awful racket. I think there was a drum and possibly a fiddle of some kind, but I am not sure as they were drowned out.

The costumes were gorgeous, made of brightly colored cloth with lots of embroidery, lace, and braid. To change scenes, the prop boys would go right out on the stage and go to work — the play never stopping. When an actor wanted to gallop off on a horse, he would grab a stick with tassels on it, swing his right leg up over it, give a kick, and gallop off. When they wanted to get in a boat, a boy would run out with a paddle, hold it up and the sailors would run to it, hop and sail off. The more the actors whirled and twirled, the better the audience liked it. All the feminine parts were played by male sopranos. The interpreter said it was a bona fide Chinese opera and some of the players were professional actors. I really got a kick out of it.

Kashmir It Was!

By April 1945 construction and improvement of the Ledo Road, now officially the Stilwell Road, was complete. The engineering units spread out along the road were involved in maintenance work, which was much less demanding during the dry season. Rest leaves were being allotted to numerous officers and enlisted men. Lieutenant John A. Power and I drew a 20-day leave. John was the battalion's Assistant Adjutant, a devout Catholic who, prior to the war, had considered becoming a priest. He was a bright, conscientious, gentleman, with an engaging sense of humor. We got along famously.

We asked where we were to go on our leave and were told we could choose any rest camp destination in the entire India-Burma Theater. There were dozens of alternatives, but we decided to go for broke. That narrowed the candidates to three: Nepal — the home of Mt. Everest; Darjeeling — the preeminent British summer retreat with a spectacular view of 28,000-foot Mt. Kanchenjunga; and the fabled Vale of Kashmir. Upon checking we found that Nepal was closed to all foreigners with the single exception of a few designated British officers who served as liaisons between the British Raj in Delhi and the King of Nepal. Darjeeling was north of Calcutta, and accessed by a stunning ride in a small, rickety train. Kashmir was a legendary valley nestled in the Himalayan mountains, but 2,000 miles away. Why not? Kashmir it was!

Our Leave: Myothit to Kashmir

The numbers along the Himalayan mountain range are the elevations, in thousands of feet above sea level, of the peaks at that location. Forty peaks have elevations of 20 thousand feet or higher, and 15 of these are 25 thousand feet or higher. The range extends for 1,500 miles and in places is 200 miles wide.

KEY

Travel by Air ——→ , Rail —|—|— , Road ═══╪═══

Scale: One inch equals 220 miles

John Power and William King. 1875th Battalion camp, Myothit.

A Fascinating Adventure

We planned to fly to Delhi and from there take a train to Rawalpindi, in what was then a part of the Punjab but is now in Pakistan. The last leg of the trip would be by British lorry over a flank of the Himalayas into Kashmir.

Our route from Calcutta through Delhi to Rawalpindi followed the legendary Grand Trunk Road. For centuries the teeming masses of India, invaders, and traders on the Silk Road had followed this route. It extended 1,300 miles from Calcutta, northwest along the Ganges River plane, through the holy city of Varanasi on the Ganges, past Agra, home of the Taj Mahal, through Delhi to Lahore and Amritsar in the Punjab, and through Rawalpindi to Peshawar on the Afghanistan border and the famed Khyber Pass.

We were driven to Myitkyina and after a six-hour wait caught a plane to Calcutta. We spent the night there and the next morning were lucky to get a plane to Agra. I recounted the rest of our journey in my letters of April 15, April 24, and May 12:

> Rather than sweat out a plane to Delhi, we hopped on one of the Indian trains — it had a dining car, a rarity in India, and served a good meal. We planned to spend the night in Delhi, but the U.S. Rail Transportation Officer said, "Uh-Uh, we didn't have orders to stay in Delhi and anyhow there was a train leaving for Lahore in one-half hour." There were four of us in a first class compartment. One was a beturbaned Indian plutocrat who had his manservant dress him, even to tying his master's shoelaces. The other was an Indian officer. We took the two empty leather benches and had a fairly good night's sleep.

A meal stop en route to Kashmir.

We arrived in Lahore in the morning, had breakfast at the station and caught a train to Rawalpindi, arriving there at eight in the evening. The next morning we arrived at the British army compound at 8:00 a.m., as instructed, only to find that the truck had left at 7:00 a.m. for Kashmir. We were wandering around the town when a civilian on a bicycle stopped to chat with us. He was an American, a Mr. Stewart, had graduated from Geneva College, near Pittsburgh, and was a professor at the Presbyterian Missionary College in Rawalpindi. He invited us to tea at 4:00 p.m. There we met his brother and a Mr. and Mrs. Cummings. The Cummings had graduated from Westminster College, also near Pittsburgh, and for a time had lived in Pittsburgh's North Side. It was an enjoyable visit.

The next morning we got up in time to catch the British lorry at 7:00 a.m. The lorry was a typical British Army truck with seats for 12 in the back and enclosed by a tarpaulin. We had two Sikh drivers who were pretty good, and quite careful. They had to be. I never saw such a road. Shortly after we started, the road climbed up the side of a mountain. It was a hard-surfaced, one-way road with sufficient room, including the shoulders, for two trucks to pass — usually. On the left was a wide, desolate, and semi-arid river valley with spectacular vistas of mountain ranges on the far side. Occasionally as we approached a blind turn, the driver would veer to the outside of the road, just in time to pass an oncoming vehicle. On each such

A scene from the road to Kashmir, after leaving Rawalpindi.

occasion we were sure we would slam into the on-coming vehicle and careen off the road into the valley far below. It was a nippy morning, but nice and sunny and not too uncomfortable.

We climbed to an elevation of 6,800 feet then down we went some 3,000 to 4,000 feet until we came to the Jhelum River Valley. This river starts in Kashmir and churns its way through towering rock gorges. Our road threaded along the sides of the gorge, mostly hewn out of solid rock, and often through rock tunnels. Its curves were so sharp that often we could see only 100 to 150 yards ahead. The road literally hung to the rock cliffs and occasionally we came to places where it tired of hanging and had washed out. We held our breath, leaned toward the uphill side and squeezed through. Or else the hillside above had collapsed, covering the road with rock. There were gangs of natives all along the road keeping it open and improving it. All the crushed rock in that 200 miles had to be crushed by hand, using small hammers. The scenery was dramatic; deep, winding gorges, precipitous mountains, and rugged snow-capped ranges in the near distance.

That afternoon it started to rain and we were up around 5,000 feet again. Boy, was it cold! The wind blew through the truck as though it were a wind tunnel. We had no gloves, light cotton socks and low-cut shoes. Luckily I had my wool uniform, field jacket, and raincoat so I didn't quite freeze to death. When we came out into the village of Kashmir we were wet, cold, and tired and all we could see was fog and a half-drowned countryside. We didn't know whether to leave in the morning, or wait a day.

The Jhelum River Valley.

A Kashmiri shikara.

The lorry took us to the billeting office, located in a reasonably modern hotel along a wide boulevard bordered on one side by an arm of the Dal Lake. At dusk we entered the hotel. It was bright, warm, attractive and filled with fashionably dressed British men and women. Prior to our trip, we had made reservations to stay in one of the houseboats moored on the Dal Lake. But we were tired and chilled to the bone. I asked the billeting officer if we could change our reservations to the deliciously warm and comfortable hotel. He said we could, but advised us to at least visit the houseboat before making our decision. His manner was such that we decided it was at least worth a try. He took us outside and introduced us to the steward from our houseboat and the shikara paddler. The Kashmiri shikara is their version of a Venetian gondola, but with a top to provide shelter from rain.

We boarded the shikara and paddled across the bay of the Dal Lake to the far side where an impressive row of houseboats was moored. It was a chilling, misty night. We docked, were led to our houseboat, crossed the covered porch and stepped dubiously inside. Gad — what a beautiful apparition! We were in a warm, cozy beautifully furnished living room. It was just like a nice house at home; oriental rugs, paneled walls and ceilings, a couch, lounging chairs, chairside tables, a writing desk, pictures, several vases of flowers, curtains, lamps, and a small bookshelf. In that one minute we felt like human beings again.

The living room led to the dining room, furnished in a similar manner. The dining room had a big, round table in the center, a buffet, and a china cupboard displaying dishes and cutlery on the shelves. Past that was the pantry and then three bedrooms, each with twin beds and a bath. The beds were gloriously long and had ample sheets and blankets. The bathrooms were a bit tricky — a mirror, an enameled basin in a rack for a wash bowl, two pitchers and a boy who brought hot and cold water, a galvanized iron tub for bathing, a potty and a bucket in a stool for a toilet. Everything was strictly hand operated, but as long as it was the help's hands we didn't mind. The kitchen was in a separate boat tied up alongside ours.

Shortly after we got there we had supper. It included a delicious roasted quail, parsleyed potatoes, fresh carrots and peas, and roasted apples and cream for desert with coffee served later in the living room. The cooking was superb and did we eat! Each day we had our choice of menu options for the following day.

All the rooms had fireplaces and were spacious and beautifully furnished. There were large windows on both sides of the boat. We had a gracious and attentive staff of five, plus the owner of the houseboat and a shikara and crew — ours alone. All meals were included. Our package price for all of this was 11 rupees a day for each of us — $3.60. Later they managed to wangle some generous tips. We firmly concurred with the billeting officer's recommendation and settled in for a luxurious stay.

Our Kashmiri houseboat and staff.

This picture was taken in 1987 when I returned to Kashmir with my wife Carol. Houseboats in the center foreground.

The Vale of Kashmir is like a gigantic cup. The Vale is relatively level, and contains numerous lakes interlaced with a network of canals. There are extensive and lush farms, scattered villages and the capital city of Srinagar. Surrounding the Vale are impressive foothills. Just beyond these the high Himalayan peaks rise and are plainly and spectacularly visible in clear weather. Unfortunately during this trip the high cloud cover denied us this view. The weather during our stay was generally cloudy, often misty with scattered rain, but pleasantly warm.

Our chief form of transportation was our shikara. We traveled through the canals and lakes, enjoying the sights on land and aboard the many cargo-laden shikaras. Activities included aqua-planing in one of the lakes, a bit of horseback riding, and hiking on some of the local hills.

Most impressive were the famed Shalimar Gardens. "Pale hands I love beside the Shalimar, Where are you now, who lies beneath your spell?"[1] There are three large gardens, each on a plateau slightly above and overlooking the lakes and the valley. They are attractively laid out, and contain elaborate rest shelters, fountains, and cascading pools. It was too early in the spring for many of the flowers to be out. At their best these gardens would be a magnificent and romantic sight. When we

[1]The *Kashmiri Song*, by Laurence Hope.

A typical native Kashmiri shop.

were there they appeared to be somewhat run down due to lack of attention, possibly because of the war and greatly reduced tourism.

We spent time shopping and window-shopping. Taking our shikara and a guide from the houseboat staff we visited many stores. The owner-merchants frequently had a propensity for colorful names such as "Suffering Moses" and "Subhana the Worst." There was a wide variety of goods available: fur hats and gloves, embroidered wool capes and scarves, lovely oriental rugs, jewelry, artistically decorated papier-mâché boxes, ornately carved wood boxes, and nests of tables. The wood used was from the local chinar tree, a lovely tall spreading tree with leaves like a maple leaf and wood like walnut. The wood carvings, papier-mâché boxes, and oriental rugs were made with superb craftsmanship and artistry, many being of museum quality and relatively inexpensive.

Whenever we went on a shikara trip merchants in their shikaras came alongside and graciously tried to interest us in their wares. Merchants would also come to our houseboat, and in such numbers that we had to have our staff turn them away. We were probably the only "rich American officers" in Kashmir at that time so we were fair game.

There was one merchant who caught our fancy, Subhana the Worst, and we had him visit our houseboat several times. He had exquisite goods, and was a master at luring the customer. He was very low-key, gracious, and knowledgeable about his goods. He would start out by showing an item, leave it in view, place a stunning counterpart nearby — saying nothing, then show a third similar item of moderate quality and describe it in some detail. Of course I then had to ask him about the prime item and he would, a bit hesitantly but very convincingly, tell me. He set the price highest for the prime item, but never too high. I bought quite a few things from him — and cherish them all to this day.

There is an interesting footnote to Subhana. In 1987 our friends, Bill and Peggy Menges and Pete and Jane Hanna, and my wife Carol and I made an extended trip to India. The Menges and Kings took a side trip to Kashmir. We stayed in a houseboat in almost the exact location as in 1945. I looked up Subhana. We located his grandson who owned a restaurant in Srinagar; he invited us for lunch. His grandfather had died some years before our visit. The grandson showed us a book featuring a number of "Fabled Merchants of the Orient." One chapter was devoted to his grandfather and I fully concurred with the author's assessment of him.

The receipt for a set of stunning cabochon rubies.

Subhana the Worst: truly a fabled merchant of the Orient.

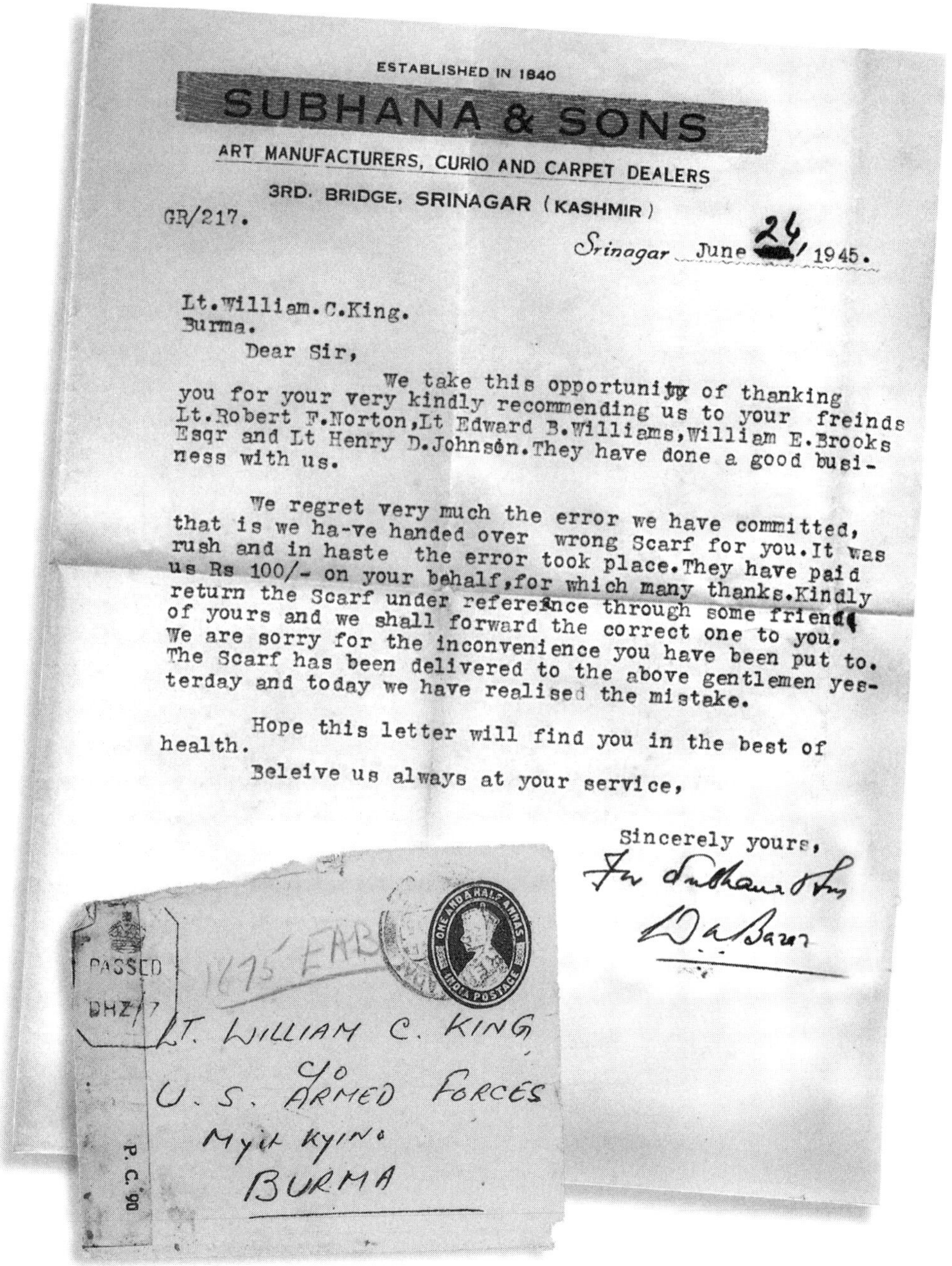

ESTABLISHED IN 1840

SUBHANA & SONS

ART MANUFACTURERS, CURIO AND CARPET DEALERS

3RD. BRIDGE, SRINAGAR (KASHMIR)

GR/217.

Srinagar June 24 1945.

Lt.William.C.King.
Burma.

Dear Sir,

We take this opportunity of thanking
you for your very kindly recommending us to your freinds
Lt.Robert F.Norton,Lt Edward B.Williams,William E.Brooks
Esqr and Lt Henry D.Johnson.They have done a good business with us.

We regret very much the error we have committed,
that is we ha-ve handed over wrong Scarf for you.It was
rush and in haste the error took place.They have paid
us Rs 100/- on your behalf,for which many thanks.Kindly
return the Scarf under reference through some friend
of yours and we shall forward the correct one to you.
We are sorry for the inconvenience you have been put to.
The Scarf has been delivered to the above gentlemen yesterday and today we have realised the mistake.

Hope this letter will find you in the best of
health.

Beleive us always at your service,

Sincerely yours,

For Subhana & Sons
D. a. Bazn

PASSED
DHZ/7
P. C. 90

1675 EABS

LT. WILLIAM C. KING,
C/o
U.S. ARMED FORCES
Myit Kyina
BURMA

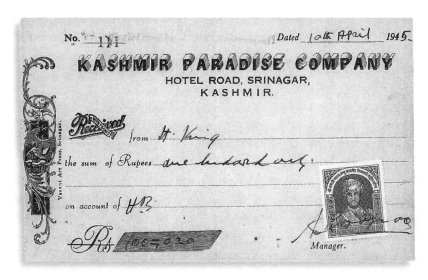

We paid more in tips than we did for the houseboat, including accommodations, meals, and staff.

Finding Our Way Back

John Power and I stayed in Kashmir about ten days; by the end of that time we felt we had seen and done most of what we could. The return trip retraced our previous journey, by truck over the awesome road to Rawalpindi, and by train from there to Delhi. We arrived in Delhi in the morning and, choosing to ignore our not-so-favorite rail transportation officer, proceeded to the officers' transient quarters in New Delhi to wash up and rest. On May 12 I wrote:

> For lunch we went to a very swanky restaurant named Piccadilly. It was just like the Rainbow Room or the ballroom in New York's Waldorf Astoria Hotel, nicely decorated, air conditioned, potted ferns, beautifully set tables, and even an orchestra playing nice dinner music. What food, whee-oh! I had cold consommé, steak and French fried potatoes, fresh peas and a chocolate sundae.

> We took the train from Delhi to Agra, arriving in the evening. John had not seen the Taj Mahal so we spent the next morning there. It is still as beautiful as ever. We went back to the Agra air base and tried to get a ride to Calcutta. We were told we just wouldn't be able to get a ride, period. We had had enough of Indian trains for awhile so we scouted around the airbase and happened to bump into a pilot who was flying to our old base in India. We thumbed a ride with him and arrived at that base just in time to miss the shuttle to Calcutta. The next plane left the next morning from a field 15 miles away. We got out on the road and thumbed our way there. The outfit there was getting ready to move so had no accommodations for us, but obliged by putting us up in an enlisted mens' barracks for the night. The next morning we caught a plane to Calcutta. After a lot of searching we managed to get a billet through the Army, but it wasn't luxurious. It consisted of a cot in a room in a private home. There wasn't much privacy for there were nine other cots in the same room, all sardine style.

> The next day we went to the base to check on plane rides back to our outfit. We were told very obligingly, "There are no planes for the next two weeks, take the train." We had taken that train from Calcutta to Ledo and had no interest in repeating that experience. That day was the next to last day of our leave and AWOL was staring us in the face. If we took the train, we would be two days late, but we would be sure of getting there. If we stayed in Calcutta, Lord only knows how late we would be. We stayed, that train ride was too awful.

Having nothing to do, that afternoon we took the Red Cross sightseeing tour of Calcutta. It was quite interesting. We saw the famous Jain Temple, the burning ghats, a decrepit museum, and the place where the Black Hole of Calcutta[1] had been.

The next morning we went to a small field outside of Calcutta and inquired about plane schedules. Again we hit it lucky (it was about time), and got a ride on a shuttle plane. It took us to some out of the way place in the middle of Assam. There we were, no plane out until the next day and we weren't sure of a ride on that. That made us one day AWOL so far. But I remembered my mother had written that one of my Carnegie Tech fraternity brothers, Bob Dismukes, was at a base in Assam with a weather unit. So we checked around and lo and behold this was the base and there was Bob, as big as life. We had a great time reminiscing about the old Tech days.

We stayed at the transient quarters and they did me wrong. We had dinner at the mess hall. Bob proceeded me and John followed me through the cafeteria line. We each had the same food. After dinner I got a severe case of stomach pains. Boy was it rough! It felt as though Patton's whole Third Army was holding maneuvers in my stomach. I finally got out of bed and staggered around until I found the dispensary. I told the medic to do something drastic as I was dying. He said, "Oh don't worry, that's just ptomaine poisoning, every one gets it here." I was given some medicine, which in a few hours worked wonders. I never did figure out how I could get so sick and Bob and John have no problem at all when all three of us were served concurrently from the same containers.

The next day we checked about a plane and were told, "Sorry, no luck." That made us two days AWOL. That meant another day of just sitting around, trying to pass the time. The following day we were desperate and did everything but get down and pray. The plane came in and went out, but this time we were in it. We were greatly relieved. I didn't mind being AWOL as much as I minded sitting around in that forsaken hole. We finally got to our home base and got a ride back to camp. We told our commanding officer about our trials and tribulations and he just laughed. He told us not to worry about it, that there wasn't much going on anyhow, and we might just as well have stayed away for a week. Visiting Kashmir was a great experience, but the trip back was not. The next leave I take will be Stateside.

[1] In 1756 there was a battle in Calcutta between British and Indian troops. British prisoners were locked up overnight by the Indian soldiers in a room 14 feet wide and 18 feet long. A number of the British died of suffocation. The room has been called the Black Hole of Calcutta.

Can It Be Kept Open?

In March and April 1945 the U.S. and Chinese forces drove the Japanese out of Lashio. Concurrently the British and Indian forces driving south in western Burma through Mandalay and along the Arakan Coast[1] forced the Japanese back to Rangoon, which fell in early May. This ended the Japanese presence in Burma.

No account of the Burma Campaign would be complete without mentioning the role Dr. Gordon Seagrave and his staff played in providing vital medical aid to the U.S. and Chinese forces. From the publisher's foreword of Dr. Seagrave's book, *Burma Surgeon Returns*:

> In the remote wilds of Northeast Burma, long before the war threatened, Dr. Gordon Seagrave was carrying on his own war against misery, disease, and death. Born in Rangoon, he was the fourth generation of his family to serve as an American missionary — and the first to be a doctor. ... His hospital [in Namkham, on the Burma Road just west of the Chinese border] was a little frame building, his equipment a wastebasketfull of broken-down surgical instruments salvaged from his training at Johns Hopkins. ... His nurses were native women from the Karen, Shan, Kachin and other tribes. Their charm and gaiety were in striking contrast to their efficiency in every direction — from giving intravenous injections to driving trucks.

---

[1] The Arakan Coast is the western flank of Burma, extending north from the capital city of Rangoon, along the eastern shore of the Bay of Bengal, towards the Indian border.

When the Japanese invaded Burma in 1942, "Dr. Seagrave was commissioned a major in the U.S. Medical Corps, formed a mobile medical unit, organized an emergency ambulance service, and put field hospitals where they were needed. Through the days and nights of Japanese bombing, he and his nurses cared for the wounded amid the flames of burning towns, moving back as the onslaught grew fiercer." He, his medical unit, and a polyglot mixture of refugees joined General Stilwell in their 300-mile retreat through the jungles of northern Burma to Imphal, India. This was an epic struggle with few supplies, along narrow trails through dense, disease- and insect-infested forests, across rivers and high mountain ranges. Much of the journey was on foot.

In the fall of 1943 General Stilwell initiated his campaign to drive the Japanese south out of Burma. The initial strike forces were followed by the engineer units building the road. Major Seagrave's medical unit accompanied the strike forces and set up temporary field hospitals at every battle site from Shingbwiyang to Namkham: through the fiercely contested battles of Hukawng Valley, Tingkawk Sakan, Jambu Bum Pass, Shaduzup, and Warazup, to the 70-day siege at Myitkyina and three-month siege at Bhamo, and finally to the battle of Namkham. The unit was frequently exposed to enemy fire, but unceasingly provided critically needed medical care to the wounded and those who contracted one of the many prevalent diseases. During this campaign the native nurses were highly efficient; they worked endless hours, ignored danger, and boosted moral with their enthusiasm. After the war the Seagrave Hospital at Namkham was rebuilt and put back into operation.

VE Day, May 8, 1945, made a big difference to the Allied troops in China, Burma, and India. Now it was clear that the combined might of the Allied forces could be brought to bear in the invasion of Japan, bringing World War II to an earlier conclusion.

In May Lieutenant General Sultan, Commanding General of the United States Forces in the India-Burma Theater, issued an order authorizing the 1875th Engineer Aviation Battalion credit for battle participation in the Central Burma Campaign, as announced by the U.S. War Department's General Order 28, 10 April 1945. This entitled all of the active officers and enlisted men in the battalion to wear a second bronze star.

The delivery of supplies to western China was assured with Japanese resistance in Burma ended, the Ledo-Burma Road in operation, airlifts

The Japanese had used Dr. Seagrave's Hospital for a fort. It was severely bombed during the war, but later rebuilt. Above and bottom left, Dr. Seagrave is seen amidst the rubble. His Burmese nurses are shown below on the right.

Photos courtesy of U.S. Army Signal Corps.

from Myitkyina to Kunming increasing steadily, and the rail line from Rangoon to Lashio about to be reopened. The road required only ongoing maintenance. Rumors started flying madly as to the next assignments for the U.S. forces in India and Burma. This continued into the summer and involved many credible and incredible alternatives. One of the more credible assignments for the 1875th was that we would be sent to the large island of Hainan, off the southeast coast of China, to build more airbases there.

In China, Burma, and India a point system was instituted for selecting veterans to return to the U.S. One point was awarded for each month of service, and a second point for each month overseas. Five points were given for each battle star, and additional points for being married, having children, etc. Eighty-five points were required for transfer home. I had 48, including credit for the two battle stars. I was one of the two youngest officers, had no service prior to Officer Candidate School, and was not given credit for service at the school since we were technically civilians while there. It would be a long time before I headed Stateside.

As long as there were Japanese in China, the Ledo-Burma Road would have to be kept open. Chiang Kai-shek's forces needed to be supplied, even though he was hoarding a significant portion of the supplies for use, after Japan's defeat, against the Chinese Communists. During the dry season little effort was needed to maintain the road. The many free hours were taken up with sports, occasional hunting, improving living quarters, writing home, and playing bridge — endless hours of bridge.

In June some natives in a nearby village developed bubonic plague. All personnel in the battalion were given immunization shots. The disease was confined to the native population and controlled there by immunization.

Later in the month intermittent squalls heralded the onset of the monsoons. At first they provided a welcome relief from the heat, but then the rains came more often and stayed longer. Being the Assistant S-3 it was my job to drive daily the 80-mile roundtrip of the section of the road for which the battalion was responsible. I inspected all the bridge abutments and culverts for erosion and the road for washouts, mudslides, and blocked ditches. Any maintenance work needed was relayed to the appropriate company or to the Chinese work battalion.

IMMUNIZATION REGISTER
AND OTHER MEDICAL DATA
(SEE AR 40—210)

NAME (LAST, FIRST, MID. INITIAL)

KING, WILLIAM C   ASN   0-511656

Date of Birth	Race	Blood Group	Med. O
11 Aug 21	W	A	

SMALLPOX VACCINE

Date	Type of Reaction	Med. O
24 Sept 45	Vaccinoid	CCJ

TRIPLE TYPHOID VACCINE

Dates Each Dose	Med. Off.
14 Feb 42 Series Completed	
24 Sept 45	CCJ

TYPHUS VACCINE

Dates Each Dose	Med. O
Series Completed 28 Nov 43	
24 Sept 45	CP

AST STARTED 15 Februar

TETANUS TOXOID

Dates Each Dose	Med. Off.
23 Oct 43	CCJ
16 Nov 43	CCJ
7 Dec 43	CCJ
21 Apr 44	CWJ

CHOL

Dates Eac
Series
28 Nov
24 Sep

YELLOW FEVER VACCINE

Date	Lot No.
10 Dec 43	AB 255

W.D., A.G.O.
Form 8-117
15 August 1944.

This Form supersede
September 1942 whi
after receipt of this

OTHER IMMUNIZATIONS

Type	Date	Lot No.	Amount	Med. Off.
Influenza	11 Dec 45		1.0 cc	HHH
Plague	12 Jun 45		0.5 cc	CP
Plague	22 Jun 45		1.0 cc	CP

SPECTACLES

Place of Refraction	Date	Glasses Required
		Yes ☐ No ☐

V.A. With Glasses   V.A. Without Glasses

d	ou	od	os	ou

	Sphero	Cylinder	Axis	Prism	Dec. In.
od	$\angle$425	$\angle$250	85		
os.	$\angle$175	$\angle$225	100		
Add.					

Bifocal Segment

Height	Inset	P.D.	Frame
mm.	mm.		Bridge Eye Size Temple
			23 43 x 3954

Position of Eyeglass Gas Mask M-1 :   Size of Gas Mask :
Commercial Type No. of Prs.   Eyeglass Gas Mask M-1
Date Ordered   Date Issued   Date Ordered   Date Issued

DENTURES

Type	*	Dates inserted if made in service
Full Upper		
Full Lower		
Partial Upper		
Partial Lower		

* Check if present when inducted or ordered to active duty.

DRUG OR SERUM SENSITIVITY

Drug of Serum	
Date or Reaction	
Type of Reaction	
Severity	Med. Off.
Remarks :	

Cres.—322 5.

Lieutenant King's immunization card: all immunizations were required, and included smallpox, typhoid, typhus, tetanus, cholera, yellow fever, influenza, and bubonic plague.

In midsummer the rains poured down for an entire week. Every rivulet, creek, and river was filled with a rushing, churning torrent of angry, brown water. We just huddled in our pyramidal tents waiting for a let-up. Working on the road was impossible. When the rains finally stopped, we found the bridges all in good condition. However, a significant portion of the culverts, all of which were four to five feet in diameter, had experienced such huge flows of water that they had popped out of their embankments like corks out of a champagne bottle. In addition, landslides had blocked the road near each end of our section. We worked furiously to bulldoze away the slides. The dislodged culverts were replaced with two of the same size, and in some cases three, and their headwalls reinforced. Our food and supplies were running short. For a while it looked as though we might have to have supplies air-dropped to us, but we were able to reopen the road before that was needed. The following weeks were fully occupied with continuing repairs and regravelling.

Then came those momentous days in early August 1945 when the whole world and our future changed completely. On August 6 the first atom bomb was dropped on Hiroshima; on August 9 the second on Nagasaki; and on August 14 Japan unconditionally surrendered. We heard the news by radio. The war was over; we were headed home!

The Corps of Engineers

They have a song about the Army, the Navy and Marines,
They have one for the Air Corps, the whole damn works, it seems,
But they've never taken the trouble tho we've served them all for years,
To even write a verse or two for the Corps of Engineers.

We build their roads and airfields, their pipe lines and their camps,
From underground munition dumps to concrete loading ramps,
Railroads, dams and bridges, electric power lines,
Canals, docks and harbors, even coal and iron mines.

But the Engineers aren't kicking, for when the Army's moving in,
We know it's just another place where we've already been.
Before the Army got there we had to break
And build it all to suit their needs, solid, safe and sound.

"If the Army and the Navy ever look on Heaven's scenes,
They will find the streets are guarded by the United States Marines."
Now who will walk the streets we aren't supposed to say,
But we offer this suggestion if they look at things that way.
When the Marines have taken over in the land that knows no year,
They'll be glad to find it was all designed by the Corps of Engineers.

The Voyage Home: Calcutta to San Francisco

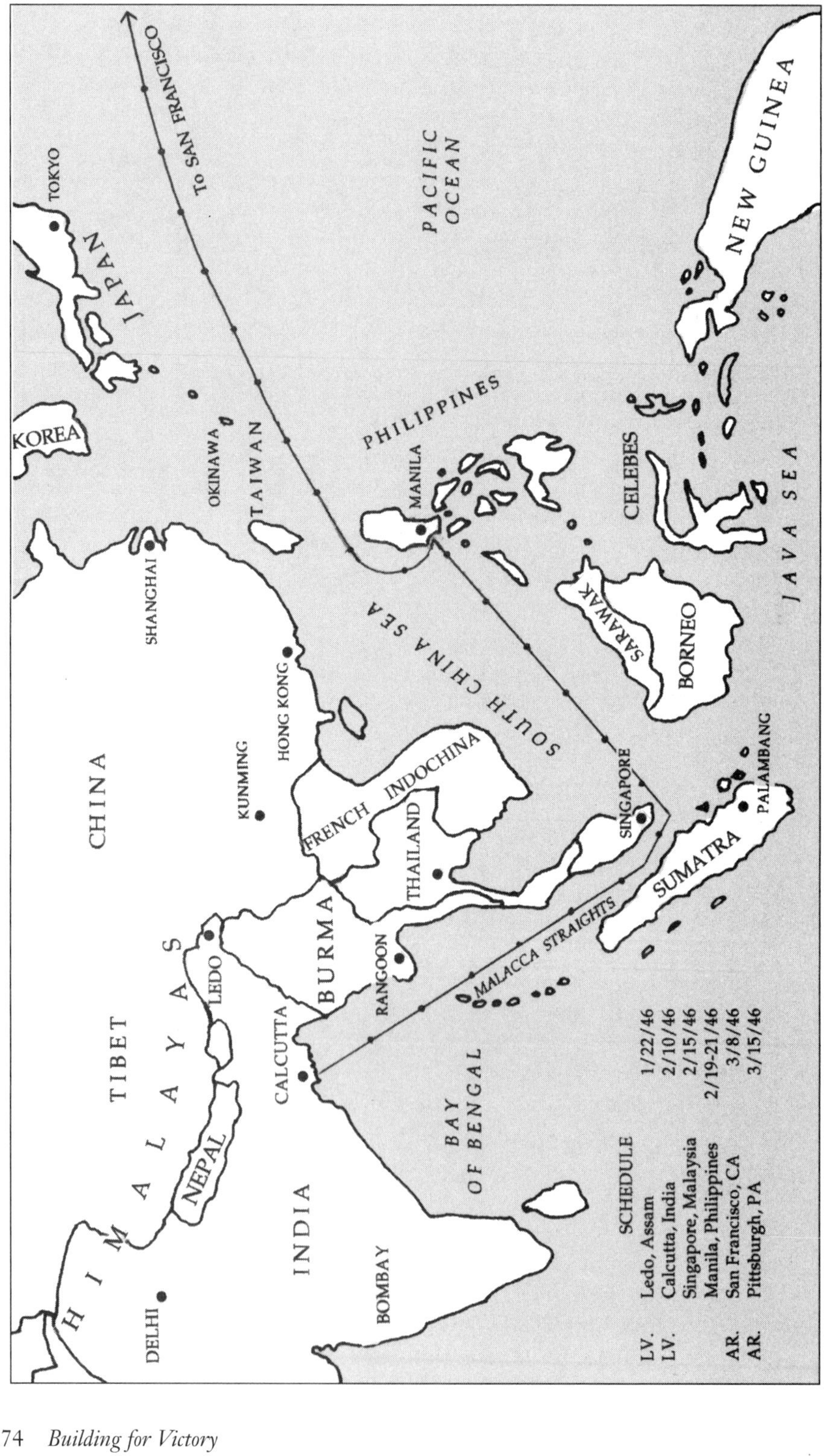

To SAN FRANCISCO

PACIFIC OCEAN

TOKYO

JAPAN

KOREA

OKINAWA

TAIWAN

SHANGHAI

CHINA

HONG KONG

KUNMING

TIBET

H I M A L A Y A S

NEPAL

DELHI

BOMBAY

INDIA

LEDO

CALCUTTA

BURMA

RANGOON

FRENCH INDOCHINA

THAILAND

BAY OF BENGAL

SOUTH CHINA SEA

PHILIPPINES

MANILA

SINGAPORE

MALACCA STRAIGHTS

SUMATRA

PALAMBANG

SARAWAK

BORNEO

CELEBES

JAVA SEA

NEW GUINEA

	SCHEDULE	
LV.	Ledo, Assam	1/22/46
LV.	Calcutta, India	2/10/46
	Singapore, Malaysia	2/15/46
	Manila, Philippines	2/19-21/46
AR.	San Francisco, CA	3/8/46
AR.	Pittsburgh, PA	3/15/46

The Long Journey Home

We would be heading home, but the question was when. I wrote to my parents on August 13, 1945: "At least with the end of the war we can start to count the days when we go home. I feel that we should be home within eight months after the war is over, but that is just a hunch." Little did I realize how prophetic that hunch was to be.

On August 16 I wrote:

> The Commanding General in Burma gave a radio talk last night and said that the War Department would announce its discharge policies in a few days and then our [Theater] Headquarters would assign priorities and let us know when we could expect to go home. Preference would go to the units with the longest time overseas, and that puts us up toward the top. Also the Ledo Road would be closed shortly and since we were near the southern end we should stand a chance of getting out fairly early. I wouldn't be surprised if we were on our way home by November, but I don't think I'll make it for Xmas.

In mid-August all the officers and men who were over 38 years old, or who had 85 points or more were reassigned for repatriation to the U.S. I had just turned 24 and had 52 points. This resulted in our losing three officers, one of whom was Major Stevenson, the S-3 and my boss. I was sorry to see him leave, but he did say to let him know, anytime after the war, if I wanted a job in the Texas Highway Department. Another officer to leave was the Battalion Supply Officer, or S-4. Thereupon I was designated the Battalion S-4. This was in addition to my Assistant S-3 duties, but these were now essentially nil. I knew very little about the S-4 job, but the remaining S-4 staff was excellent and this would require that I spend time in Ledo, a welcome respite from the jungles of central Burma. The authorized rank for Battalion S-4 was captain, but with the war over all promotions were frozen.

It was obvious that the battalion was going home. To clear for repatriation, we were required to document and account for all of the equipment and government property we had been issued. What we had would be turned in to the Quartermaster Depot. For any lost or damaged property we had to fill out forms detailing why and how it was lost and damaged and why it could not be recovered or repaired. This was a massive administrative job, given all the vehicles, heavy equipment, arms and housekeeping facilities we had.

In early September Advanced Section Headquarters in Ledo ordered the battalion to return to a site on the road immediately east of Ledo and at the foot of the Patkai Mountains. There we were put to work repairing monsoon damage to the road, particularly in the treacherous Pangsau Pass area. This relocation was a boon to our supply activities since it put us less than an hour's jeep ride from Area Headquarters and the Quartermaster Depot.

In mid-September I wrote:

> They have been keeping me really busy, and I do mean busy.
> We have taken over a stretch of the Road from one of the outfits
> that is going home and are having to take over all of their equipment
> and checking it. In all I have signed for over a half a million dollars
> worth of equipment in the last two weeks. This involves a lot of
> traveling around and I've gotten to know half of the people on the
> base by now. I'm sure that just about the time that we get everything
> taken over and all the records straight I'll have to start turning every-
> thing in for our battalion — I hope! I am clearing all my records as
> soon as possible and will have all the records ready — I'm deter-
> mined the Supply Section will not hold up the battalion when it
> comes time to go home.

About that time the Advanced Section Headquarters came to its senses. It issued a regulation stating that within a specified period of time units could account for and obtain a release on any lost or damaged equipment by simply listing it on a form stating that it had been lost or damaged in the line of duty and having the form signed by the unit commander. This obviated a large administrative load.

Within a day or two I had those forms completed, taken to Headquarters, and formally accepted. This regulation was the only practical alternative, since it had become clear that all of our equipment, except for arms, were to be left behind and given to the Indian or British authorities or sold at bargain level prices to the local people. It just was not economical to try to repatriate all of this and the soldiers. It soon became a common sight to see ecstatic natives careening down the road "driving" a jeep or truck with the top down, with their white-muslin clothing flapping in the breeze, happily waving at onlookers, as long as the tankful of gas lasted.

Since all of the trucks and construction equipment were to be left behind, the local entrepreneurs were desperately in need of skilled personnel having the expertise to repair, maintain, and operate the machinery. They offered attractive salaries to American military personnel about to be repatriated, if those individuals would stay in India and take such jobs. The salary offers reached $20,000 per year, an unheard-of level at that time. The catch was that the pay would be in rupees and the Indian Government would not permit rupees to be converted in India to dollars for expatriation to the U.S. The only way to get the money home was to buy and export Indian goods. I never heard of any takers.

By late September, thanks to the point system, we had lost between 150 and 200 men and were down to nine officers out of our allotted 29. John Power was now Adjutant (Personnel Officer, S-1). He and I were the two busiest officers by far. Then he went to the hospital with appendicitis and I became acting Adjutant for a brief time. We were the two youngest officers, and therefore would be the last to leave and were the logical choices for the assignments vital to processing for repatriation.

Early in October the battalion was relieved of its duties in maintaining the road and intensified preparations for returning home. Departure was indicated for the middle of the month. This was soon deferred. American military personnel were being moved out of China on an expedited basis because of the revolution there. The delay in repatriation was compounded by the lack of ships to take the troops Stateside. As a result Karachi, the nearest port to the U.S., was jammed with waiting troops, as were the transit camps at Chabua and Ledo. In mid-October we turned in all of our equipment and supplies and I took all of our supply records to the staging area for inspection, processing, and

Our battalion movie theater, also used for Sunday church services. Courtesy of 1875th Battalion.

approval. We passed with flying colors.

The delay in shipping out to the U.S. gave us the most pleasant interludes we had during our stay overseas. Lieutenant Tullson, my tent mate, and I had installed a wooden floor in our tent, framed and netted it in, and arranged it with a bedroom and living room. We had steel cots with mattresses, a worn but attractive oriental rug in the living room, indirect overhead lighting, and an electric fan. Beer, Coke, and ice were plentiful and we had movies several times a week. Frequently after the movies our gang of officers would congregate in our tent, since it was the most deluxe in the battalion.

We had Wednesday and Saturday afternoons off and all day Sunday. I could only take advantage of that when we had all our equipment turned in and our records cleared. We could eat at the mess for our battalion, at the mess for transient officers, and at two very good Chinese restaurants in Ledo. There was dancing at the Officers' Club two or three times a week, thanks to the ample number of nurses.

Regularly at about 4 p.m. a group of officers would gather on the veranda of the nurses' quarters in Ledo, enjoy cold drinks, and socialize. The fall weather was reminiscent of beautiful Indian summer days at home. We developed a close-knit camaraderie. All of us had had the experience of our lives in China, Burma, and India. While it lacked the drama and importance of Normandy or of the island-hopping combat of the Pacific, it involved an important job under difficult conditions, and had been a job well done. Now we were relatively carefree and about to be scattered to all corners of America. Almost daily we would bid good-bye to some of our group at the airport or train station; soon others would fill their places. It was a magical moment, frozen in time for a few short weeks, a moment to be nurtured and savored to the fullest.

Sabotaged!

All of this came to a sudden halt for me when, in late October, Headquarters issued orders that all officers with less than 65 points would be screened out of units to be repatriated and would be reassigned. I had less than 65 points and was reassigned to the 45th General Service Regiment, currently stationed 103 miles south on the Ledo Road at Shingbwiyang. Back into the jungle, what a blow!

It was a difficult day when I said good-bye to my remaining comrades in the 1875th. We had been together for two and one-half years and shared so many memorable experiences. The battalion left Ledo by train in two sections on November 10 and 13. After an exhausting eight-day trip across India it arrived in Karachi. Three weeks later the battalion embarked on the USS *General C. C. Ballou*. The *Ballou* sailed

The 1875th Battalion boarding the train in Ledo for the long trip home through Calcutta and Karachi to New York. Staff Sergeant Arthur P. Gariepy is looking out of the train window.
Courtesy of Edward Gariepy.

back through the Indian Ocean, the Suez Canal, the Mediterranean and across the Atlantic Ocean, arriving in New York on New Year's Day. The battalion was deactivated immediately after debarkation.

Just before leaving Ledo I wrote to my family:

> Upon joining the 45th G. S. Regiment, I hope to be assigned to the supply section. I like the work, have learned something about it in the past few months, and know all the ropes in Ledo, and all of the people connected with supply. Also, there is a deal worked out that if I get into supply I can be assigned to Ledo on detached service, which is but strictly a good thing. Some of the 45th officers are working on this for me as is the Engineer supply officer here in Ledo.

On October 27 I climbed into my jeep with my footlocker, drove the 103 miles to Shingbwiyang, and reported for duty. The Commanding Officer was Colonel Greenlee whom I had met previously; we got along well. He was a huge man, perhaps 6'5" tall, 280 pounds, and all muscle. The 45th had white officers and black enlisted men. To my delight I was assigned as regimental Supply Officer.

The regiment was maintaining the road, but the weather was good and the workload light. It would not be long before the 45th would be slated for repatriation so I once again initiated the process of preparing all the supply records needed when that time came. There was one interesting incident. One day I noticed an enlisted man walking around with the entire top of the toe of each shoe cut off. I asked him why. He said that he wore size 15-triple-E shoes and that he had not been able to get any since he arrived in India. He had to use smaller shoes and the only way to make them work was to cut the top of the toe off of each shoe and let his toes hang out. On my next trip to Ledo I spent hours scouring through the quartermaster warehouses and finally found not one but two pairs of size 15-triple-E shoes. I gave them to him back in camp, he tried them on, and, looking at me with the biggest grin I have ever seen said, "Sir, you just done worked a miracle!" I had a friend for life.

During November and December I made trips to Ledo, but only when necessary for my supply duties. The trip was too grueling to make it more often. Each stay in Ledo was extended for a bit, though, for "needed rest and recreation." In early December the Colonel submitted to the Advance Section Command a recommendation for my promotion to captain. All promotions were rejected since the regiment was scheduled for deactivation on January 1. I spent my third Christmas overseas enjoying a fine Christmas dinner in the heart of the northern Burma jungle. In many ways we had much to be thankful for. But that did not diminish our collective desire to get homeward bound.

On December 28 I was granted a four-day leave to Calcutta, air travel authorized. I met a friend on the plane and we got a room in a grand old colonial hotel on Chowringhee Road, one of the main boulevards in Calcutta. Our time was spent taking in the sights and relaxing at the Officers' Club. We celebrated New Year's Eve there. They were out of champagne so my friend and I went back to our hotel room, called room service, and ordered four bottles of champagne. The wine steward delivered them and enthusiastically offered to open them. We apologized, said they were for a party outside the hotel, and left him rather crestfallen. Back at the Officers' Club the champagne was doled out in small portions and greatly appreciated.

Also on December 28 my chief assistant, Warrant Officer Junior Grade Robert S. Ascher, and I were relieved from assignment to the 45th General Service Regiment and assigned to the 76th Ordnance Base Depot, Panitola India. The 76th was a transient personnel holding unit located near Ledo. This meant that the long journey home had started. Bob Ascher was a fine young man and had been a great help to me. Although we had been reassigned, we stayed on temporary duty with the 45th to wind down their supply activities, but relocated to Ledo where most of our work was centered. This also meant that I could spend a bit more time at the nursing center veranda with my old group of comrades who still remained and with some new acquaintances.

By mid-January 1946 we had cleared up most of the 45th's supply activities. On January 17 Bob Ascher and I were relieved from temporary duty with the 45th and attached unassigned to Replacement Depot No. 3 at Kanchrapara, India, a suburb of Calcutta. That was double good news. First, we had now entered the process for going home. Second, we did not have to suffer the eight-day train ride to Karachi. This also meant we would be sailing across the Pacific and would disembark on the west coast of the U.S.

Lieutenant King and Warrant Officer Bob Ascher.

On January 23 I wrote to my parents:

We're now in the Kanchrapara replacement depot, about 40 miles from central Calcutta. This is our final camp before getting on the boat. We flew from Chabua to Calcutta in a C-54 yesterday, loaded up in the back of an army truck and were driven here. We are in tents in an officers' billeting area. There are showers, a mess, a theater and an officers' club. The food is OK.

This morning we were processed, had all our records checked and made out a bucketful of forms. Now we wait for our ship to come in. When that will be is highly indefinite. The tentative schedule was just posted, but that is changed about once a week. Moreover they ship officers according to their points and length of stay so if some high-pointers come in after I do they may get priority. There is one ship scheduled in for Feb. 7th–8th and two for Feb. 9th–10th with a total capacity of 10,000 troops. There are about 6,000 here now, with other groups due in next week. I think it's a pretty safe bet I'll make one of those ships.

There was little to do at Kanchrapara other than eat, sleep, read, play volleyball, watch second-rate U.S. movies, and wait. Occasionally I went into Calcutta for a bit of sightseeing and relaxation at the officers' club. On one such trip I met an attractive English girl. I had a few dates with her, took her to Firpo's restaurant, *the* restaurant in Calcutta, for a sumptuous dinner, and to several horse races. Her family often attended the races. At one I noticed that a British enlisted man came up, spoke to her father, a British Colonel, and the two immediately left. I asked my date what had happened. She replied that British officers were not allowed to attend the races during duty hours, even if they had no work to do, and that an inspector had been spotted in the stands writing down the names of any British officers he saw there. Her father's name escaped the list.

There was one very disturbing development during this period. We received word that a number of officers with less than 65 points and with the appropriate qualifications were to be sent to Shanghai, China for a minimum of six months. I had fewer than 65 points and very likely had the appropriate qualifications. I had absolutely no interest in an assignment in China, especially with a revolution going on. There was only one place I wanted to go and that was home.

Because of this possible development, my following days became hectic. This is best conveyed by quoting almost verbatim my letter of February 9 to my parents:

This may well be the last letter I write to you from Indian soil. Tomorrow [Sun. Feb. 10, 1946] I'm scheduled to leave here at 10:30 a.m. and load directly onto the Army transport, the USS *General Haas*. It is due to sail the day after tomorrow (Mon. Feb. 11th) — 21 days to Seattle, arriving Mar. 4th.

You probably noticed I said "this *may* well be the last letter." Although my information is official, the events of the past two weeks have left me so skeptical that I'm not going to believe I'm on my way home until the boat is moving out to sea with me on it. In the past few letters I have written to you and said that all we were doing was loafing and taking it easy. That was a lot of baloney. I haven't told you what was actually going on because there was no use driving you crazy by building up your hopes and tearing them down with incessant promises and contradictions.

Following is a brief recap of the past two weeks. As you know, we got here on Jan. 22nd, processed on the 23rd, and expected to ship on Feb. 5th to 8th. Well, on Saturday, Jan. 26th we were in Calcutta visiting some friends and heard rumors about surplus officers going to China. I thought the boys there were feeding me a line so on Sunday morning, Jan. 27th, I checked at the base and found out it was true — surplus officers would be offered to China. I was surplus and very offerable! I checked some more and found neither Calcutta nor Kanchrapara here had submitted our names; I felt fairly safe.

Now starts the maelstrom. About Wed., Jan. 30th, I saw the adjutant from our ordnance outfit in Panitola. He was visiting Calcutta and said they *had* sent our names in to be offered to China! We crossed our fingers and hoped. Thursday, Jan. 31st in the afternoon they had a meeting of all the transient officers and a permanent party major from the base here told us what the score was on living conditions, processing and priorities in shipping. One statement he made was that once you were on a shipping list you were *definitely* on your way home. Once the shipping order had been cut, no one would be taken off. I spent Friday, Feb. 1st in Calcutta and got back about midnight, and there was my name on the bulletin board — Lieutenant Wm. C. King (and about 300 others) to ship on the *General Haas*. I almost blew up from sheer joy. And after what the major had said we all bid China goodbye.

Sat. Morning, Feb 2nd at breakfast instructions were posted that all of us on the *Haas* would process immediately to clear the base and would leave at 1:00 p.m. for camp Dakuria — the staging area in Calcutta where troops are billeted just prior to boarding a ship. At about that time, the company commanding officer of the replacement company here called me in and said that the base commanding officer wanted to see me in reference to a traffic violation. I had been charged with speeding back in Ledo and the charge had finally caught up with me. Boy did I sweat. Usually traffic violators are called up by the General and that takes days and days of red tape. So I had awful visions of not making the boat. Well I must have an honest face because the base commanding officer just bawled me out and restricted me to the base until I was to sail, which was that afternoon.

I zoomed back to the company area, cleared and had just started to pack when the public address system announced that all persons scheduled to leave on the *Haas* would stop clearing immediately. We couldn't imagine what the reason was. Naturally there were thousands of rumors, there always are. On Sunday nothing happened. On Monday, Feb. 4th orders came out deleting some 250 of us from the shipping list — still no reason, but the China deal looked grimly imminent. To be so close — two and one-half hours to go for embarkation — and to be snatched back for another six months in

China would be hard to take. Soon we learned that all men not eligible for discharge by June 30th were liable for duty in China. The officers would be picked by specialty number, a number designating one's specific military qualifications. Mine was one of the ones they would probably want and there were only a handful of ground forces officers here, the majority being Air Force officers, for which there is no demand.

The criteria for separation by June 30th are 42 months service or 65 points. I would have neither, so it looked like China here I come. No person could have felt as low as I did. I had one faint hope, if I could get credit for my three months of OCS service I would only lack seven days of active service and might be able to swing a deal. So I went to base headquarters and they said they would look into it for me. On Thursday I went into Calcutta and talked to the major in charge of the personnel section. I had known him in Ledo, he had screened me there for transfer to Kanchrapara, and I asked him about the China deal. He asked me if I would have 30 months overseas time by June 30th. I said yes, 30 months and two weeks. He said "you won't go to China." He had just received a radiogram stating that anyone with 30 months of overseas service as of June 30th would be eligible for separation and *not* be sent to China! I was so happy I almost hugged him.

This morning, Sat. Feb. 9th, I went to headquarters and checked on my OCS time and, glory be, they said OK, so I got my personnel records and had them changed — I now have 63 points and 36 months service as of Jan 6th. I then went to the records section, and had them make out a Change-of-Data form. I had them include a change in my specialty number from Supply, which is pretty much in demand, to Airport Engineer which was my old one and should not be needed much now. The Change-of-Data form had to go to the outbound records section so they would have the right data in making up my shipment orders, when and if. To make sure the form didn't get lost I took it over myself. While there I overheard a sergeant talking about getting a roster of officers with enough time overseas so I talked to him, had him get my card and include the new data. He said I would be on the *General Bliss*, due to sail the end of next week, Feb. 16th. I felt good.

This afternoon about 4:00 p.m. I was sitting on the porch of the Officers' Club reading and the public affairs system told me to report to the orderly room. I did. They said I should be ready to leave at 10:30 a.m. tomorrow morning (Sun., Feb. 10th) and go directly to the *General Haas*, which is due to leave Monday. I was flabbergasted, but not for long. I had to clear and pack and write this letter, all by 10:00 a.m. tomorrow. I took my physical, cleared my mess bill, ate supper, and packed. First thing tomorrow I clear Supply, the Post Exchange, get my money changed, and take off.

But — due to my past experiences I am still being careful. I will give this letter to Bob Ascher, my supply assistant and a grand guy, tomorrow, Sunday, Feb. 10th, and tell him if I don't call him by Tuesday morning, Feb. 12th, to mail it. If I do call him, something has happened and not to mail it. So if you get this I should be on a ship just starting home. On Feb. 13, 1944 we pulled into Bombay Harbor. It looks as though I'll leave Calcutta on Feb. 11, 1946 or just two days short of two years in India and Burma.

On February 16, 1946 I wrote to my parents the following — my last letter to them while overseas:

Well, I guess I'm going to make it this time, for I'm writing this on a table in our stateroom aboard the *General Haas*. We're plowing through the waters of the South China Seas, so it's America the Beautiful, here I come. Every time I think of it I feel so good I just glow all over.

My last letter, which you should have by now, brought you up to Saturday evening, Feb. 9th, the day prior to my embarkation. I'll continue from there. Sunday morning I finished clearing the base, and by 10:30 a.m. you can bet your boots I was ready. We hopped into a command car and drove to Calcutta, arriving at the docks at about 12:30 p.m. There the fellows checking the passengers onto the boat had no record of me. But the sergeant who drove us down verified the fact that I should be there, and I knew one of the captains working there so I was authorized to embark. We walked onto the dock, and boarded a launch that took us to the ship. The ship is an Army transport about 500 feet long and 17,000 tons. It is much larger than the Liberty Ship on which we crossed the Atlantic, but not as big as the British liner we took from Algiers to Bombay.

The port of Calcutta is 80 miles up the Hooghly River from the Bay of Bengal and our ship could only navigate the river at high tide, so at 12:45 p.m. we sailed. The river is quite narrow at the port so we had to back down a couple of miles and then some tugs turned us around. Down the Hooghly we went, taking a last look at Calcutta. Tuesday morning we were in the Bay of Bengal. Wednesday morning we passed the northern Andaman Islands and headed for the Malacca Straights. Friday morning we entered the Straights and at about 7:45 p.m. Friday evening we rounded the tip of the Malay Peninsula and sighted Singapore, all lighted up like a Christmas tree. Now we're heading through the China Sea. Our only stop will be in Manila where we will re-provision and then head for Seattle.

The boarding pier with the General Haas *in the background.*

Packed in like sardines, but no complaints.

The three photographs courtesy of the U.S. Army Signal Corps.

Sailing down the Hooghly River.

Transport General W. F. Haas *passes under the Golden Gate Bridge on her arrival in San Francisco: March 8, 1946.* Associated Press Wirephoto.

En route our destination was changed to San Francisco. We sailed under the Golden Gate Bridge at 8:00 a.m. on March 8, 1946, 26 months and 26 days after we had sailed out of Hampton Roads, Virginia. It was a beautiful, sunny morning and glorious in every way. We spent the night at Camp Stoneman outside of San Francisco and the next day entrained for home. I noted that my Certificate of Service did not give me credit for the three months spent in OCS, but my Separation Qualification Record did. Both included a promotion to the rank of Captain in the Army of the United States, effective March 15th. On that date I was officially relieved from active duty, with 70 days of accrued terminal leave, through May 25th.

A good deed, beautifully rewarded: dinner in Chicago with Bob Ascher's wife.

From San Francisco I took a train to Chicago and stayed overnight. There I visited the family of Lieutenant James D. Liston. He was a young officer in the 45th Regiment, with whom I had worked and who had not yet been scheduled for repatriation to the U.S.

That evening I took Bob Ascher's wife to dinner at the Bismarck Hotel. I had been close to Bob, owed him a favor for mailing my letter to my parents, and wanted to assure her he was fine and would be home soon.

The next morning I boarded a train to Pittsburgh and was met at Union Station by my parents. It was a heartfelt reunion for all of us. I returned having lost 30 of my 165 pounds abroad due to the searing climate and recurring dysentery, but soon regained my full weight.

Conversation Piece

**IS THE GATEWAY TO INDIA AT BOMBAY
REALLY AS BEAUTIFUL AS THEY SAY?**

Don't rightly know, Ma'am. Did my part
Breakin' point in the jungle's heart;
Blasted the boulders, felled the trees
With red muck oozin' around our knees,
Carved the guts from the Patkai's side,
Dozed our trace, made it clean and wide,
Metaled and graded, dug and filled:
We had the Ledo Road to build.

**WELL, SURE YOU SAW A BURNING GHAT,
FAKIRS, ROPE-TRICKS, AND ALL OF THAT.**

Reckon I didn't. But way up ahead
I tended the wounded, buried the dead.
For I was a Medic and little we knew
But the smell of sickness all day through,
Mosquitoes, leeches, and thick dark mud
Where the Chinese spilled their blood.
After the enemy guns were stilled:
We had the Ledo Road to build.

**OF COURSE YOU FOUND THE TAJ MAHAL,
THE LOVELIEST BUILDING OF THEM ALL.**

Can't really say, lady. I was stuck
Far beyond Shing with a QM truck.
Monsoon was rugged there, hot and wet,
Nothing to do but to work and sweat.
And dry was the dust upon my mouth
As steadily big "cats" roared on south,
Over the ground where the Japs lay killed:
We had the Ledo Road to build.

**YOU'VE BEEN GONE TWO YEARS THIS
SPRING, DIDN'T YOU SEE A SINGLE THING?**

Never saw much but the moon shine on
A Burmese temple around Maingkwan,
And silver transports high in the sky,
Thursday river and the swift Tani,
And Hukwang Valley coming all green,
Those are the only sights I've seen.
Did our job though, like God willed:
We had the Ledo Road to build.

* * * *

In early 1945, while still in Burma, I had decided that immediately after my discharge from active duty I would attend graduate school and obtain a Master's Degree in Chemical Engineering. Much progress had been made in that field during the war, and I needed both to catch up with those developments and to refine my skills. During the following months, through correspondence with my father, the initial steps had been taken to apply for entrance to the Massachusetts Institute of Technology, MIT. Immediately after returning home my application was finalized and accepted. I entered graduate school at MIT in early June 1946. In December 1947 I graduated with a Master's Degree in Chemical Engineering Practice and started what would become a successful 37-year career with the Gulf Oil Corporation, spent largely in Pittsburgh. A year later, December 1948, I met Carolyn O. Thorne who would become my wife. We have a fine marriage, and a large and loving family including four married children, their spouses, and 13 grandchildren.

It is probable that some of this would have turned out differently if I had been sent to China by the Army in early 1946 and returned home toward the end of that year, or later.

Opposite: Sergeant Smith Dawless describes the experiences of many American soldiers who were less fortunate than I. Courtesy of The Office of Public Relations, USF in IBT (India-Burma Theater).

Higashikuni: Japan's Prince and Premier. Courtesy of Associated Press.

In Retrospect

In late June 1944 the B-29s started flying from India to bomb Japan. Due largely to the extreme length of this flight, the military impact on Japan was nominal, although the psychological impact was significant. In early 1945, the B-29s were relocated to the Marianas Islands in the Pacific Ocean, where they were within easy range of Japan. After the war, Prince Higashikuni, Commander in Chief of Japan's Home Defense Headquarters, told Allied interrogators that the arrival of the B-29s in the Marianas had for all practical purposes put an end to his nation's hope for victory. He said, "We had nothing in Japan that we could use against such a weapon. From the point of view of the Home Defense Command, we felt the war was lost and we said so."[1]

In the spring of 1946, the U.S. Army abandoned the Ledo and Burma Roads. In mid-1946 David Richardson revisited the Ledo Road. He flew from an almost deserted Chabua airfield to Myitkyina. There he found the mammoth pontoon bridges across the Irrawaddy River shredded by recent monsoon floods. In the hills north of Myitkyina the irrepressible forests were rapidly encroaching. All the big bridges and gaping sections of the road had been washed out, and low sections covered with landslides. The Allies' engineers had maintained the road through the summer of 1945; without them the road was helpless to withstand nature's onslaught.

[1]Keith Wheeler and the editors of Time-Life Books, *Bombers Over Japan — World War II.*

Stilwell Road Abandoned by U.S.

WASHINGTON, March 9 (UP)—
The Stilwell Road and 11 airfields in Burma have been abandoned because they are useless for anything but war, the Government announced today.

The road and the fields were carved out of mountains and jungles at a money cost of about 164 million dollars with the labor and skill of thousands of U. S. troops and Chinese workers, the Foreign Liquidation Commission said. Their abandonment, the FLC said, will expedite the return home of more than 12,000 American soldiers.

Explaining that salvage of either the road or the airfields would cost more than it would be worth, the commission added:

"There can be no better example of the terrific waste of war and the fact that much war surplus cannot be used in the civilian economy."

Was the enormous effort to establish ground access from India to China justified? I believe it was. There were hundreds of thousands of Japanese troops in China during the war. In July of 1945 there was a massive movement of Allied troops, principally American, across the Pacific Ocean in preparation for the invasion of Japan, scheduled for November of that year. It was important that the Japanese troops in China be kept there so they could not return to Japan and make the invasion even more difficult. Maintaining a well-supplied Chinese military force and U.S. Air Force in China were key factors in accomplishing this.

The test of the atom bomb at Alamogordo, New Mexico did not take place until July 16, 1945. Had this test failed, and had that resulted in a delay in the successful development of the bomb, the invasion of Japan would certainly have taken place. This could have resulted in hundreds of thousands of American casualties, and millions of Japanese casualties. The Japanese soldiers were willing to fight to the death for such remote Burmese towns as Bhamo and Namkham; they would have done so for their homeland.

Bibliography

Belden, Jack, *Retreat with Stilwell*, Alfred A. Knopf, New York, 1943.

Buchanan, S/Sgt. C. M. and McDowell, Sgt. John R., *Stilwell Road*, Office of Public Relations, USF in IBT, Advance Section, 1945.

Coe, Douglas, *The Burma Road*, Julian Messner, New York, 1946.

Eldridge, Freed, *Wrath in Burma*, Doubleday & Co., Garden City, N.Y., 1946.

Gibson, Hugh, *The Ciano Diaries, 1939–1943*, Doubleday & Co., Garden City, N.Y., 1945.

Hibbert, Christopher, *Mussolini*, Ballantine Books, New York, 1972.

Hoyt, Edwin P., *Japan's War, The Great Pacific Conflict*, McGraw-Hill Book Co., New York, 1986.

Jackson, Carlton, *Forgotten Tragedy, The Sinking of HMT Rohna*, U.S. Naval Institute Press, Annapolis, MD, 1997.

King, William C., Letters Written to His Family, 1943–1946.

King, William C., U.S. Army 201 Personnel File, 1943–1946.

Morrison, Wilbur H., *Birds from Hell, History of the B-29*, Hellgate Press, Central Point, OR, 2001.

Moser, Don, and the editors of Time-Life Books, *China, Burma, India — World War II*, Alexandria, VA, 1978.

Power, Lieutenant John A., *"ESSAYONS" — History of the 1875th Engineer Aviation Battalion*, 1946. **Copies of *"ESSAYONS"* may be obtained from the Senator John Heinz Pittsburgh Regional History Center, see page iv.**

Seagrave, Gordon S., M.D., *Burma Surgeon*, W. W. Norton, New York, 1943.

Seagrave, Gordon S., M.D., *Burma Surgeon Returns*, W. W. Norton, New York, 1946.

Slim, Field-Marshall Viscount William J., *Defeat into Victory, Battling Japan in Burma and India, 1942–1945*, Cooper Square Press, New York, 2000.

Thomas, Lowell, *Back to Mandalay*, The Greystone Press, New York, 1951.

Tuchman, Barbara W., *Stilwell and the American Experience in China, 1911–1945*, Bantam Books, New York, 1971.

Webster, Donovan, *The Burma Road, The Epic Story of the China-Burma-India Theater in World War II*, Farrar, Straus and Giroux, New York, 2003.

Wheeler, Keith, and the editors of Time-Life Books, *Bombers Over Japan — World War II*, Alexandria, VA, 1982.

White, Theodore H., *The Stilwell Papers*, William Sloan Associates, New York, 1948.

Yergin, Daniel, *The Prize*, Simon & Schuster, New York, 1991.

Appendix

1875TH ENGINEER AVIATION BATTALION
ROSTERS

The battalion was made up of men from all corners of the United States. They were predominantly white, with a few of Hispanic origin. They represented a host of ethnic backgrounds and occupations. There were architects and ditch diggers, alleged Mafioso, and an agent of Hollywood actors and actresses. Many of the men had farm backgrounds and some had just graduated from high school. Except for a few of the officers and enlisted men, all were less than 30 years old. They were a randomly selected group of Americans.

These men never did develop a burning loyalty to the battalion; to my knowledge there have been no postwar reunions. Yet they coalesced into a highly efficient, resourceful, and unified team. They knew a war had to be won, and they were determined to do their collective best in their assigned roles. That they did — in building the B-29 airbases in Bengal, India, and in building long stretches of the Ledo Road. They were not involved in combat, but were exposed to severe, and in some cases fatal, accidents and disease. They returned home with a strong sense of pride, knowing that together they had carried out their tasks superbly well.

The wreath above is the Meritorious Unit Service Award, presented to the battalion for outstanding performance in building the Dudhkundi airbase. It is gold and is worn on the right sleeve above the wrist (see photo on page 189).

1875TH ENGINEER AVIATION BATTALION

ROSTER

First Platoon, Company A

Platoon Commander: Lieutenant William Collins King

Platoon Sergeant: Greene

FIRST SQUAD	SECOND SQUAD	THIRD SQUAD
Squad Leader	Squad Leader	Squad Leader
Kanter, K. K.	Simon, L. G.	Rost, M.
Endreson, E.	Bouska, R.	Botkin, R. M.
Gasperoni, L. H.	Cardwell, M. L.	Current, O.
Irwin, C.	Culver, K.	Hayes, R. W.
Jones, E. E.	Essary	Jones, M. A.
Kort	Frabel, R.	Miller
Martin, C. E.	Haynes	Robinson, E.
Oswald, J.	Kerley, W. T.	Schaner, F.
Perkins, G. C.	Klein, A. E.	Scott
Pulver	Parker, H.	Walker, S.
Sesker, C. S.	Pusateri, A.	Wightman, T.
Smethurst	Sobieski, J.	Williams, J. W.
Swanson	Tomek, J. P.	
Tope, W. B.	Warren	
Trapp	White, A. T.	
Witt, P. A.		
Znoy, C.		

Author's note: The information for the platoon roster above appears just as it is on an original roster issued in mid-1943. Sergeant Kanter was Platoon Sergeant overseas. There were periodic changes in personnel and squad assignments.

The names and home addresses on the following pages appear just as they do on an original list issued to battalion members upon their departure from Burma in the fall of 1945. The state abbreviations have been changed to conform to current standards.

Sergeant Arthur P. Gariepy, Third Platoon,
"A" Company, 1875th Engineer Aviation
Battalion. This picture and the Battalion Roster are
courtesy of his son, Edward Gariepy.

1875th ENGINEER AVIATION BATTALION
WORLD WAR II HOME ADDRESSES

OFFICERS (listed according to rank)

Cox, Lieutenant Colonel Lavonne E.   3217 Campus Blvd., Albuquerque, NM

Burnhart, Major Vincent N.   1050 Emerson St., Denver, CO

Stevenson, Major Homer E. M.   2102 Stamford Lane, Austin 21, TX

Burleson, Captain Spencer A.   Hartselle, AL

Zimmerman, Captain Edward E., Jr.   285 W. Mission, Ventura, CA

Lieutenants

Bender, John N.   Box 66, Lanse, PA

Brooks, William E., Jr.   607 N. Dotsy St., Box 86, Odessa, TX ("A" Company)

Byers, Kenneth W.   1714 State Highway 4-N, Spring Lake, NJ

Chilton, Claude L.   1541 Glen Rd., Dayton 10, OH

Cipolla, Roland H.   984 Atwood Ave., Johnston, RI ("B" Company)

Colclough, Leo J.   AA Ambassador Apt., West Trinity Ave., Durham, NC
(H&S Company)

Drown, Ralph D.   1156 Court St., Eldo, NV

Hedden, Aaron Leslie   214 West Glen Ave., Ridgewood, NJ ("B" Company)

Hooker, Orval N.   Rolling Fork, MS

Hunt, John W.   142 Clark Place, Memphis, TN

Johnson, Henry D., Jr.   1019 S. Cherry, Ada, OK ("B" Company)

Lieutenants (continued)

King, William C.   208 Gladstone Rd., Pittsburgh, PA

Kintz, Charles O.   1825 W. Hill St., Louisville, KY (Greeley, CO)
(H&S Company)

Lamas, Joseph F.   20 Spruce St., Great Neck, NY (Medical Detachment)

Luallen, Ulyssess B.   Paris, KY (H&S Company)

Magnuson, William C.   1753 Beech St., St. Paul, MN (H&S Company)

Northrop, Seymour E.   1425 West 8th Ave., Spokane, WA

Petrie, James E.   1538 Washington St., N.E., Minneapolis, MN
(H&S Company)

Polivy, Charles   50 E. Raymond St., Hartford 5, CT (Medical Detachment)

Power, John A.   104 Moosic St., Jessup, PA

Roeder, Otto L., Jr.   2124 N. 31st, Philadelphia, PA ("C" Company)

Silverstein, Morris   1416 S. Springfield, Chicago, IL ("C" Company)

Solomon, William L.   Belzori, MS

Stultz, Darrell W.   Atlanta, NE

Tullson, Rudolph V.   99 Potter St., Cranston, RI (H&S Company)

Unger, Morris D.   1745 Grand Concourse, Apt. 10M, New York, NY
(Medical Detachment)

Williams, Edward B.   c/o Dr. W. H. Bray, Fowler, CO ("B" Company)

Warrant Officers

LaMuska, Howard D.   920 Water St., Eau Clair, WI

McWilliams, Clark   4952 McPherson Ave., St. Louis, MO

Myers, Ralph K.   Parkston, SD

Sandoval, F. Z.   312 9th St., Las Vegas, NM

The company or medical detachment assignments shown for sixteen of the above officers are those included in the original copy of the roster. Many officers were assigned to more than one company during their service with the battalion.

NONCOMMISSIONED OFFICERS AND ENLISTED MEN

H&S Company

Abbott, Cloyd G.   RR #4, Box 118, Bakersfield, CA

Ahrens, Maxie   Fredericksburg, TX

Anderson, Arnold R.   2500 East 30th, Kansas City, MO

Avin, Edward   688 Saratoga Ave., Brooklyn, NY

Bailey, Beryl H.   Hebron, WV

Baker, Roy C.   201 Poplar St., Providence, KY

Balabar, Leon C.   4184 Alabama St., San Diego 3, CA

Ball, Loyce E.   RR #1, Box 175, Gurdon, AR

Bandy, Walter J.   1451 W. Flournoy St., Chicago, IL

Bazil, Edward R.   632 Railroad St., Forest City, PA

Berkowitz, Joel   2517 Glynn Court, Detroit, MI

Blue, William L.   Fife Lake, MI

Boatman, William C.   2108 California Ave., Richmond, CA

Boswell, Coy L.   Box 125, Ballinger, TX

Bouton, Donald A.   Fransis Ave., Oeonta, NY

Bowman, Ralph W.   RR #4, Des Moines, IA

Brown, Howard E.   Rt. #2 Box 3, Santa Fe, NM

Brown, William J.   222 Orchard Lane, Edgeworth, PA

Bryant, James W.   5817 Northwest 17th Ave., Miami, FL

Campbell, James A.   308 Baker St., Longmont, CO

Cantrell, Allen J.   2125 Walnut St., Martinez, CA

Cantrell, D. E., Jr.   Well Machine & Supply Co., Ft. Worth, TX

Celia, James J.   221 No. 61st, Philadelphia, PA

Charman, Walter A.   30 Gleason St., Thomaston, ME

Chitwood, Edward L.   R #2, Wartrace, TN

Christ, Raymond   Box 145, Girard, OH

Cissell, James R.   2938 Cleveland Blvd., Louisville, KY

Clark, Hubert T.   540 So. Owasso St., Tulsa, OK

Clay, Charles L., Jr.   R6 Box 50, Charleston, WV

Cockerill, Kern L.   R #1, Box 822, West Sacramento, CA

Cohen, Aaron A. (c/o Katz)   1410 Avenue S, Brooklyn 29, NY

Cohn, David M.   177 S. E. St., San Bernandino, CA

Coker, Bobbie   2159 Alder St., Eugene, OR

Connelley, Allen J.   1120 E. Washington St., Phoenix, AZ

Cotton, Hubert C.   Reed, OK

Crites, Kenneth   RR #2, Oaktown, IN

H&S Company (continued)

Crookham, Paul E. Atwater, CA

Czaja, Peter E. East Hoosac St., Adams, MA

Dahlgren, John E. 1449 Oak Grove Dr., Los Angeles, CA

Delauranti, James 11302 S. Champlain Ave., Chicago, IL

Dell, Donald J. 64 Campbell St., Newberg, NY

DeLong, George L. 525 3rd St., San Bernardino, CA

DeMarco, Gaetano F. 165 E. 106th St., New York, NY

Demers, Joseph A. 597 Dexter St., Central Falls, RI

Dent, Frederic R. 2973 Norwood St., Columbus, OH

DeRosa, Salvatore P. #7 Bank St., New York, NY

Dickerson, Herbert L. 27 Swiss St., Warren, PA

Domecki, Bernard J. 1400 Edgewood Park, Pewaukee, WI

Douglas, Paul F. 612 So. 5th St., Chickasha, OK

Downing, Norman C. Sake St., Onancock, VA

Dreifort, Donald A. 906 Alhambra Rd., Cleveland, OH

Duclett, Joseph Spring Creek, NC

DuMarce, Harold W. 513 6th St. South, Virginia, MN

Duncan, Elwin R. Dickens, IA

Edwards, Jerry C. Cullman, AL

Edwards, Ray H. Shullsburg, WI

Ellis, Harold J. 557 Allegheny Ave., Oakmont, PA

Ellis, Howard B. Weeping Water, NE

Emmett, Robert 200 S. Elena, Redondo Beach, CA

Ensminger, Charles F. RR #3, Mercersberg, PA

Farrell, Giles G. 536 No. Kingsley Dr., Los Angeles, CA

Fellows, Lloyd F. 1401 Francis St., Jackson, MI

Fogg, Ralph H. 1906 Euclid Ave., Schenectady, NY

Forrest, Raymond C. 435 West Portage Ave., Sault Ste. Marie, MI

Frazier, Earl J. RR #2, Hillsboro, IL

Fritz, Clarence F. Park Crest, Barnesville, PA

Galassi, Daniel 1432 W. Flournoy St., Chicago, IL

Garrow, Oliver 4310 Cicotte St., Detroit, MI

Gendron, Joseph R. St. Marys, MO

Gerow, Irving F. Liberty, NY

Gifford, Roland J. 3860 Fairmount Ave., Philadelphia, PA

Giles, James M. 2508 Fifth Ave. No., Birmingham, AL

Gill, Harlis Rt #2 Box 160A, Leesville, LA

H&S Company (continued)

Gonzalez, Ruben R.   1014 Bartlett St., Los Angeles, CA

Graybill, Albert C.   611 Morrill Ave. S.E., Roanoke, VA

Guffey, James R.   Box 13, Wyona, OK

Hannah, William G.   1844 E. Mariposa St., El Segundo, CA

Hansen, Robert L.   Box 141, Bridgewater, NY

Harris, Alvis   4130 Seahorn Ave., Knoxville, TN

Harrison, James F.   Renick, WV

Hayden, James G.   3233 Walnut St. N.E., Washington, DC

Hayes, Austin P.   Thermond, NC

Hayes, Kenneth L.   Ina, IL

Henkenmeier, Loren E.   Carlinville, IL

Hernandez, Ralph Y   2627 W. Martin St., San Antonio, TX

Hickman, Byron L.   Malvern, AR

Hodgdon, Charles R.   Fryburg, ME

Holley, Hubert H.   1209 E. Lancaster, Ft. Worth, TX

Houser, Herman E.   111 Second St., Oneida, PA

Huffman, Donald L.   RR #4, Box 538, Traverse City, MI

Innes, Daniel T., Jr.   22 William St., Towanda, PA

Jacobs, Jack A.   Erie, MI

Jahimiak, Raymond J.   1920 State St., LaCrosse, WI

Janik, Steve   Dayton, TX

Jones, Bert   Lee Creek, AR

Jones, Eddie F., Jr.   4165 No. Sherman Dr., Indianapolis, IN

Jones, Wallace S.   Christiansburg, VA

Jones, William O.   Rt #3 Box 244A, Mesquite, TX

Judnich, Frederick   Box 119, Lake Linden, MI

Karasik, Max   1269 East 18th St., Brooklyn, NY

Keese, George W.   Clarkdale, AR

Kelleher, John F.   134 Englewood Ave., Brookline, MA

Ketcham, Howard S.   Otisville, NY

Kirkpatrick, John A.   4039 E. 14th St., Des Moines, IA

Koman, Allen A.   Barrington Rd., Baltimore, MD

Kommalan, August M.   922 S. Ellwood Ave., Baltimore, MD

Kramer, Edward J.,   Inwood, IA

Krepps, Robert R.   323 Ohio Ave., Wilson, PA

LaLonde, Derwood R.   511 Washington Ave., Alpina, MI

Landrum, William B.   Box 124, Ethel, MS

H&S Company (continued)

Langston, Carlos C. 1137 8th St., New Orleans, LA

Larson, Kenneth E.   1268 Elati St., Denver, CO

Lawing, Horace E.   205 Frieda Ave., Kirkwood, MO

Lear, Jack A.   RR #1, Mountain Top, PA

Lecher, Donald A.   1323 W. Groeling Ave., Milwaukee, WI

Lewellen, John K.   Frankfort, MO

Lindsey, Marvin G.   406 Stanton Ave., Florence, AL

Liput, Stanley L.   Westinghouse St., Wilmerding, PA

Long, Joseph C.   Clio, AL

Marksbury, Wesley R.   3018 Tracy St., Kansas City, MO

Mason, Larven   Box 1252, Las Vegas, NV

Maxwell, William J.   4423 Ave. R., Galveston, TX

Mayville, Richard H.,   1410 Bluff St., Flint, MI

McCutcheon, Jacob P.   R #3 Box 703, Johnstown, PA

McGrath, Thomas E.   8007 Ellis Ave. Chicago, IL

Meadows, Vernie J.   R #1, Box 143, Raven, VA

Medina, Jose   517 S. Gregory, San Diego, CA

Mengrain, Clarence J.   1584 Elmhurst, Detroit, MI

Mercer, Frank C.   3357 No. Oakland Ave., Milwaukee, WI

Mertens, Franklin J.   R #1, Rosendale, WI

Meyer, Carl J.   2202 Lane St., Fall City, NE

Micholichih, Edward   20 Espy St., Wilkes Barre, PA

Miles, Colon B.   601 Julian Ave., Thomasville, NC

Miller, Edgar D.   2260 Jennings Ave., Ft. Worth, TX

Moerk, William F.   1050 Waveland Ave., Chicago, IL

Montgomery, James R.   942 Jackson St., Denver, CO

Moore, John C.   Cameron, SC

Morgan, Thomas J.   407 Woodstock Ave., Staten Island, NY

Morrozoff, Ivan A.   1056 Progress St., Fayetteville, NC

Mueller, Sylvester A.   Box 311, Manson, IA

Murray, Keith   3101 Parkland Blvd., Tampa 6, FL

Nielson, Gordon K.   6216 S. 27th St., Omaha, NE

Onacilla, Stephen A.   5 Sission Court, Bayonne, NJ

Orr, Kenneth W.   R #4, Vinita, OK

Otto, Clement B.   2202 W. Dayton St., Flint, MI

Page, William D.   222 North "C" St., Fremont, NE

Palmer, Clarence B.   2018 Wilkins St., Saginaw, MI

Pardee, William E.   920 West Buyrys Place, Denver, CO

Parmele, Arthur F.   19 Shirley St., Shortsville, NY

Perrotto, Alexander S.   135 Niagara St., Canandaigua, NY

Pevehouse, Jack A.   South Coffeeville, OK

Peyton, Dale C.   1420 N. St. SW, Cedar Rapids, IA

Picard, Leo J.   Spring St., Amesbury, MA

Pickett, Harry T.   2937 W. Congress, Chicago, IL

Pilat, Alexander   6158 Selkirk St., Detroit, MI

Pitchell, Thomas J.   262 No. Grove St., East Orange, NJ

Porter, Merle A.   Alsace Way, Colorado Springs, CO

Postle, Martin W.   Box 64, Basco, IL

Priefert, Harley W.   Hebron, NE

Prudhomme, James W.   Box 127, Canpti, LA

Radenbuagh, Maurice E.   General Delivery, St. James, MN

Radie, Alphonse J.   1022 Wilson Rd., Fall River, MA

Rapaport, Samuel   136 W. 168th St., Bronx, NY

Ricciardelli, Vito   187 Parker St., Newark, NJ

Rinehard, Mendel L.   Leesville, SC

Rodhe, Jack K.   RD #4, Chardon, OH

Rose, George H.   1083 East 171st St., Cleveland, OH

Rusin, John T.   12223 Emerald Ave., Chicago, IL

Sammons, Darrah D.   Pelican Rapids, MN

Sankary, Abraham   1524 Cooper St., Ft. Worth, TX

Santmire, Joe C.   693 So. Ohio Ave., Columbus, OH

Scerba, Enro   766 N. Green Ave., Detroit, MI

Schwieman, Robert E.   1205 Summit St., Kalamazoo, MI

Sevillano, Bill   Artesia, CA

Sharpe, Frederick F.   66 W. Enterprize St., Glen Tyon, PA

Shauck, William C.   16 West Moreland St., Westminster, MD

Siegrist, Charles C.   7409 Michigan Ave., St. Louis, MO

Simpson, Donald C.   1941 N. Keeler Ave., Chicago, IL

Sinclair, Raymond A.   Hartford, CT

Sington, Home W.   5723 St. Lawrence St., Detroit, MI

Slagle, William E.   39 Indianola Rd., Youngstown, OH

Smith, Arthur F.   1422 N. Pacific, Glendale, CA

Smith, Raymond R.   RR #10, Box 978, Tacoma, WA

Smith, Trenton L.   1202 N. Main St., High Point, NC

H&S Company (continued)

Solomon, George W.   RFD #3 Box 289, Uniontown, PA

Stephan, Frederick G.   R #2, Massillon, OH

Streaker, Charles W.   1158 N. Longwood St., Baltimore, MD

Stumpf, Kenneth B.   R #1, Highland, CA

Sullivan, George K.   13–3 Adams Ave., Burton, SD

Sullivan, Harold A.   Hancock, WI

Sutton, Richard H.   2214 McNair Ave., St. Louis, MO

Taylor, Linford J.   4346 St. James St., Detroit, MI

Taylor, Robert P.   R #1, Stanley, VA

Templeton, Buster B.   Madill, OK

Tenney, Joseph F.   19 William St., Walden, NY

Tester, Harold   RR #1, Nickalosville, KY

Tharp, Garland H.   1734 Prospect Ave., National City, CA

Thompson, Junius H.   AuSable Chasm, NY

Tomschin, Clarence L.   "Da Sveed from Minn"

Trute, Clifton L.   Hustler, WI

Tucker, Ellis L.   2116 W. Baltimore St., Baltimore, MD

VanBramer, Leonard P.   33 Silver St., Norwich, NY

Vinick, Bernard S.   40 Blue Hill Ave., Hartford, CT

Vitale, Thomas S.   27 Lafayette St., Milton, MA

Walker, Hazel   RR #1, Casar, NC

Warren, George S., Jr.   309 S. Washington St., San Angelo, TX

Warren, Joseph N.   984 New York Ave., Huntington Station, Long Island, NY

Warriner, Rudi A.   317 ½ Highland Ave., Beloit, WI

Weaver, Robert L.   1104 N. Confederate St., Tyler, TX

Webb, Giles B.   Lakeland, GA

West, Albert L.   Box 61, Opekiska, WV

Wiggins, Robert L.   293 East Fulton St., Columbus, OH

Wilhite, Charles C.   Cortez, CO

Wingren, Clyde T.   1806 West 8th St., Austin, TX

Wolcott, Warren W.   414 East 2, Spokane, WA

Wolfe, Joseph G.   4420 Beta Ave., Cleveland, OH

Worley, James L.   R #1, Lacey Springs, AL

Wozniak, Stephen A.   422 Milwaukee St., Grand Rapids, MI

Young, Harold M.   412 Kearney Addition, Nebraska City, NE

Ziemer, Harry W.   Matherville, IL

Zimmerman, Robert P.   New Springfield, OH

"A" Company

Armand, Clyde B.   Kratz Springs, LA

Augustynowitz, John   402 Hermit St., Philadelphia, PA

Bartels, Ruben   4325 S. Ardmore Ave., Villa Park, IL

Baumann, Lewis J.   902 Adana Rd., Pikesville, MD

Baumhardt, Wilfred   P.O. Box 27, Scotland, TX

Beasley, Ernest   P.O. Box 425, Odessa, TX

Berger, John   1919 Bongham St., Houston, TX

Bloore, Quentin F.   2159 E. 96th St., Chicago, IL

Botkins, Ray M.   Headwaters, VA

Bouska, Robert   Tyndall, SD

Broer, Eddie F.   Randolph, NE

Brookshire, Jack D.   Route #1, N. Wikesboro, NC

Buettner, Chas. A.   1142 Washington Blvd., Baltimore 30, MD

Burkhammer, Marshall W.   1806 Marcum Terrace, Huntington, WV

Bushey, George   217 Spruce St., Albany, NY

Cambre, Jerome R.   216 Rose Ave., New Orleans 20, LA

Cardwell, Melvyn L.   1314 Pacific Ave., Tacoma, WA

Carpenter, Bertram   572 Woodrow St., Beaumont, TX

Chapman, William L.   14273 Jane St., Detroit, MI

Chillas, Carl R.   903 Landis Ave., Lancaster, PA

Convenuto, Joseph   402 18th St., Brooklyn, NY

Corley, Rance E.   1924 Cryan St., Dallas, TX
                       4924 Gryan St., Dallas, TX

Cravens, James R.   1209 N. Alameda, Las Cruces, NM

Cullen, Fredrick   23 Chesapeake Ave., Crisfield, MD

Cumby, Richard   2408 Truxillo St., Houston, TX

Current, Olna   407 N. 17th St., Omaha, NE

DiMundo, Americo   67 Russo St., Providence, RI

Diorio, Arthur   222 Palmer St., Wooster, OH

Drake, Vern D.   Route #5, Box 533, Orlando, FL

Ellison, Robert   507 Walnut St., Dowagiac, MI

Ellsperman, Lewis   Las Anumas, CO

Enderson, Edwin   911 West Pikes Peak, Colorado Springs, CO

Erkman, Wm. J.   128 Wyckoff Ave., Brooklyn, NY

Everett, Wilbur   Decatur, MS

Flynn, Kenneth   Faubush, KY

Frabel, Robert   Wausaukee, WI

Fury, Paul H.   8132 Willard Ave., Detroit, MI

Gabbard, Ray   1707 Holman St., Covington, KY

Gambrel, Albert   Pineville, KY

Gariepy, Arthur P.   Box 153, Hubbell, MI
(Please see photo and acknowledgement on page 199)

Gasperoni, Luciano H.   510 Paterson Plank Rd., Union City, NJ

George, Loren   2151 ½ Canadian St., Vinita, OK

Gonzales, Eloy J.   1710 New Mexico Ave., Las Vegas, NM

Goree, Leslie W.   Currenville, MO

Goughf, Charles   R. R. #1, Leesburg, AL

Green, Paul   Box 46, Stockton, KS

Griffin, James A.   Route #1, Kokomo, MS

Gustin, George   Addenville, PA

Guthrie, Ray   Allison, TX

Hamel, Edmund   7605 Beacon Ave., Seattle, WA

Harrach, Russell   Grant, NE

Hart, Alfred B. L.   Versailles, MO

Haverkamp, Gordon   Detroit Lakes, MN

Hawk, Donald   Mitchell, IN

Hays, Ralph W.   Oilton, OK

Hedinger, Charles   3744 Drummond St., E. Chicago, IL

Heidtbrink, Warren H.   Malcom, NE

Hendricks, Luther   416 N. 4th St., Sterling, CO
330 Elm St., Sterling, CO

Hendrickson, Harold R.   75 Adelaide St., Rochester, NY

Hensley, Ira A.   1835 3rd St., N.E., Apt. 45, Washington, DC

Hibbard, Omar   6030 Stone Island, Chicago, IL

Hill, Glen W.   P.O. Box 533, Chelsea, OK

Holman, James   618 12th St. N.W., Apt. 107, Washington, DC

Howard, Luther   Baxter, KY

Inman, Carlton   2518 Longstreet Ave. S.W., Grand Rapids, MI

Irwin, Charles   4819 3rd Ave., Los Angeles, CA

Jaeger, Lester V.   3926 Melbourne St., Houston, TX

Jenkins, Cleo A.   613 North St., Sparta, WI

Johnson, Paul E.   325 Jackson St., Warren, PA

Jones, Ernest E.   9310 Lowell Ave., Cleveland, OH

Jones, Maurice A.   1802 Washington St., Kansas City, MO

Jordan, Glen E.   1522 Lafayette, Denver, CO

Kanter, Kenneth G.   Brillion, WI

Kaura, Charles E. Rockville, NE

Kelley, Jack W. Box 167, Baynton, OK

Kerley, W. T. Box 282, Melrose, NM

Klein, August E. 281 Forest Hill Dr., Youngstown, OH

Krey, Clarence 6603 Fern St., Detroit 10, MI

LeRoy, Harold C. 172 S. Main St., Liberty, NY

Levonavich, Alfred J. 495 Lincoln Ave., Brooklyn, NY

Malley, Albert C. 410 Fern St., New Castle, PA

Maloney, Francis 700 Strand, Redondo, CA

Martin, Clarence E. 867 Aqua Fria, Santa Fe, NM

McDow, Arthur Quitman, LA

Miller, Edgar 2260 Jennings Ave., Fort Worth, TX

Miller, Milum D. Kingspore, TN

Neal, Harvey J. 179 Glade St., Muskegon, MI

Nethington, Donald G. 6714 Sura St., Bell Gardens, CA

Oest, John Box 671, Ingleside, TX

O'Neill, Ray Randolph, NE

Osterman, Wesley Kilgore, NE

Oswald, Joseph R.D. #2, Chicora, PA

Palmer, Harold L. 228 W. 4th St., Spokane, WA

Palmer, John A. Glenham, NY

Pangione, Anthony A. 6810 Durham Ave., North Bergen, NJ

Parker, Hubert 1411 E. Garnett St., Gainesville, TX

Parker, Raymond L. Winston-Salem, NC

Parkinson, Kenneth W. 1126 Wesslesley Ave., Steubenville, OH

Perkins, Gordon C. Route #2, Box 42, Norfolk, VA

Platt, Irving 242 83rd St., Brooklyn, NY

Prleant, Alfred Route #3, Campbell, MO

Pusateri, Anthony 97–11 75th St., Ozone Park 17, NY

Raverkamp, Gordon Detroit Lakes, MN

Rayner, Jack R. Route #1, Box 792, Tacoma, WA

Rice, Harry R. D. #2, Beaver Dams, NY

Rich, James R. Rockford, AL

Riemer, Sam 2550 East 153rd St., Cleveland, OH

Ritzer, William C. Mine Hill, Ozford, NJ

Robinson, Edward 2823 Lucas Dr., Dallas, TX

Rost, Myron R. R. #1, Box 59, Chamois, MO

Schaner, Francis 908 ½ 1st St., Villa Park, IL

"A" Company (continued)

Schittino, John A.   1517 66th St., Brooklyn, NY

Schlafer, Maurice   Burbon, MO

Segrest, John C.   Port Gibson, MS

Serna, James   Box 176, Espanola, NM

Sesker, Oscar S.   1123 W. 85th St., Los Angeles, CA

Sforza, Emanuel   828 Oak St., Syracuse, NY

Shattuck, Francis D.   12 ½ Seminary St., Auburn, NY

Shearer, Luther (Decon)   Dade City, FL

Sheffield, Willie M.   281 23rd St., Brooklyn, NY

Shephard, James   Route #1, Bolling, AL

Sherry, Francis J.   3119 33rd St., Astoria, Long Island, NY

Simon, Louis G.   R.F.D. #1, Aurora, OH

Sobieski, John   31 Park St., Hartford 6, CT

Sobol, Norman   10630 St. Clair, Cleveland, OH

Standley, Dean M.   R.F.D. #2, Revure, MO

Stark, W.   2628 Campbell St., Kansas City, MO

Suttle, Delbert   R.R. #1, Gardner, IL

Tate, Edward   Star Route #2, Seagraves, TX

Taylor, Walter E.   2302 S. Early St., Kansas City, KS

Tomek, John P.   122 Highland Ave., Byesville, OH

Tope, Willard B.   285 Lennoz Ave., Columbus 4, OH

Tratchel, Donald   418 N. 4th Ave. E., Newton, IA

Turner, Earl C.   Route #1, Pelham, NC

Walker, Sammie   Phoenix, AZ

Wallace, C. B.   701 Hays St., Kerrville, TX

White, Alfred T.   111 Heflin Courts, San Antonio, TX

Wightman, Thomas   2906 Strawberry Lane, Port Huron, MI

Williams, Maxie D.   2410 Park Ave., Norwood 12, OH

Williams, Roger   4503 River Ave., S. Charleston, WV

Wilmoth, Grady   Route #2, Portales, NM

Wilson, Woodrow   R.D. Box 231, Prague, OK

Witt, Paul A.   602 19th Ave., Fulton, IL

Woolridge, John R.   319 W. Market St., Clearfield, PA

Yanochko, John   125 Main St., Mary D, PA

Youngerman, Arthur C.   10 S. Bell Ave., Springfield, OH

Zagami, Frank J.   561 Broadway, Somerville, MA

Zbin, Stephen J.   281 Forest Hill Dr., Youngstown, OH

Znoy, Charles   P.O. Box 1105, Weirton, WV

"B" Company

Adams, Earl M.   Route 2, Harlingen, TX

Albert, Wesley W.   Coodys Bluff, OK

Anderson, Carl R.   1241 Evelyn St., Berkeley, CA

Bacon, Ross A.   c/o C. A. Bacon, Box 665, Silver City, NM

Bailey, Elmo E.   2800 Clovis Street, Bluefield, WV

Beauprie, Willard L.   6910 S. Michigan Ave., Chicago, IL

Bednoschek, Ray A.   690 West 19th St., Eugene, OR

Beecher, Russell B.   327 East Maple St., Beaver Dam, WI

Bento, Humberto C.   291 Portland St., Cambridge, MA

Black, Robert R.   South 2nd St., Oregon, IL

Bolin, Clarence E. W.   46 Newton St., Bridgeport, CT

Britz, Walter J.   260 North Bluff St., Joliet, IL

Brodbeck, Clement R.   121 South Perry St., St. Marys, OH

Bullock, Sanford H.   c/o Roth Typesetting Co., 211 High Ave., Cleveland, OH

Burke, Francis E.   Box 206, Lakeside, CA

Buss, John F., Jr.   2610 West Lincoln Ave., Milwaukee, WI

Butcher, Robert C.   53 Donnybrook Rd., Brighton, MA

Butts, Howard E.   211 Wallace Ave., Pennwood Farms, Wilkins Twp.,
East Pittsburgh, PA

Caldwell, William   Route 4, New Albany, MS

Carvajal, Rafael R.   P.O. Box 1212, Yuma, AZ

Catona, Joseph S.   12115 S. Eggliston Ave., Chicago, IL

Chamberlain, Harold O.   Fort Bridger, WY

Chappell, Robert E.   Route 3, Marten, TN

Clark, Kenneth L.   228 West Lynde St., Watertown, NY

Clarke, William B.   c/o Lewis Shaw, Liberty, UT

Clements, Earl R.   c/o General Delivery, Corpus Christi, TX

Colson, Adren A.   Folkston, GA

Conard, Howard R.   Route #4, Box 548, Bakersfield, CA

Copeland, James L.   905 East Second St., Tuscumbia, AL

Cosenza, Joseph   333 Fourth St., Jersey City, NJ

Crain, Hugh F.   Kansas Geological Survey, University of Kansas,
Lawrence, KS

Curran, John J.   166 Palmer Ave., Syracuse, NY

Daniels, Arnold M.   R.D. #1, Mill Run, PA

Dargis, Edward J.   7121 South Rockwell St., Chicago, IL

Darnell, Willard   West 109 Euclid Ave., Spokane, WA

Davis, Gerald R.   6743 Troost Ave., North Hollywood, CA

Dillon, Richard V.   803 S. 3rd St., Pekin, IL

Ebbole, Joseph R.   832 S. Carondelet St., Los Angeles, CA

Egan, Charles R.   519 8th St., Huntington, WV

Eisenhour, John H.   R.D. #1, Palmyra, PA

Erban, George A.   74 Steele Ave., Conimicut, RI

Erickson, Leslie R.   Box 50, Plainfield, IL

Esposito, Samuel P., Jr.   313 East Dominick St., Rome, NY

Fisher, Louis J.   741 Oak St., Beloit, WI

Frazier, Orville   601 North 8th St., Rocky Ford, CO

Frederick, Clifford O.   32 East Alexis St., Ecorse, MI

Gage, Henry S., Jr.   Hitching Post Riding and Sales Stables, RFD, Johnstown, NY

Gallucci, Anthony F.   444 Villa Ave., Staten Island, NY

Gamma, Frank R.   Box 500, Ada Ave., Mountain View, CA

Gardner, Edward C.   1635 Jackson Blvd., Chicago, IL

Garretson, Laurence E.   1008 West 14th St., Grand Island, NE

Gehman, Eugene Y.   R.F.D. #2, New Holland, Lancaster County, PA

Gillespey, Kenneth H.   Box 1112, Joliet, IL

Goldstein, Irving   51–53 Glen St., Glen Cove, Long Island, NY

Goodwin, Anderson N.   Sellersburg, IN

Graham, William O.   Box 381, Whitmire, SC

Grant, Rodger C.   77 Lincoln Ave., Attleboro, MA

Green, Joseph L.   Route 3, Clanton, AL

Hall, James M.   Route #1, Box 282, Mt. Airy, NC

Harden, Isaac H.   1707 18th St., Lubbock, TX

Harrell, G. M.   Route #1, Rogersville, TN

Haynes, William H.   1653 St. Jean Ave., Detroit, MI

Heifner, Vernon K.   Route #3, Chattanooga, TN

Hendrickson, Kermit L.   512 Baker Ave., Decorah, IA

Henson, Ray   7012 Osvorn Ave., Hammond, IN

Hernandez, Jose R.   327 East Main St., San Gabriel, CA

Hill, Ralph   4 Kentucky St., Johnson City, TN

Hinkel, Elmer F.   339 McCartney St., Easton, PA

Hoerber, Walter H.   2115 ½ 2nd Ave., Los Angeles, CA

Holt, Jack T.   2419 Gass Ave., Overland, MO

Hoover, Donell   404 Harding Ave., Canton, MS

Hunter, George A.   27 McNutt Ave., Albany, NY

Kelley, Charles J.   R.F.D. #2, Box 64 B, Roby Rd., Laurel, MD

"B" Company (continued)

Kelley, William E.   208 East Grant St., Blair, NE

Kerr, Kenneth O.   Box 82, Farmington, CA

Kessler, Edward H.   6404 Avenue C, Houston, TX

Kiser, James R.   Beardstown, IL

Knott, David L.   Box 181, Burkeville, VA

Kogelschatz, Harvey E.   677 Meadow Brook, Detroit, MI

Kort, Chester E.   Box 693, San Angelo, TX

Kosalko, John F.   1743 Canal St., Northampton, PA

Krystyniak, Paul P.   6795 Mansfield St., Detroit, MI

Larsh, Melvin G.   917 Ave. I, Council Bluffs, IA

Larson, Elvin E.   Birkenfield, OR

Lassiter, Herman   439 Belmont Ave., Alexander Park, Portsmouth, VA

Lawellin, Joseph L.   Box 367, Livingston, MT

Leasure, Robert N.   1335 North River Ave., Toronto, OH

Lewis, Joseph R.   Star Route 1, Stonefort, IL

Liddy, Meredith W.   RR #3, Bluffton, IN

Lorenzo, Harold J.   525 Dean St., Brooklyn, NY

Lozano, Renaud C.   R.F.D. Box 266, Galveston, TX

Malsom, Larry A.   1649 Quince, Denver, CO

Marenda, Anthony J.   336 Butler St., Brooklyn, NY

Marston, Earle M.   2910 Keswick Rd., Baltimore, MD

McCall, Lloyd E.   112 South Elati St., Denver, CO

McColley, Clifford E.   4017 North Troy St., Chicago, IL

McCord, Ralph A.   P.O. Box 113, Sulphur, LA

McDonald, Robert D.   P.O. Box 95, Garden Grove, CA

McLaughlin, Willis I.   Modesto, CA

Meglan, Albert C.   1562 East 173rd St., Cleveland, OH

Meyers, Donald R.   563 East 7th St., Winona, MN

Michaud, Harty P.   5 Knox St., Lewiston, ME

Moore, Clarence E.   Route #1, Americus, KS

Morris, Willie A.   RR #1, East Bernard, TX

Mullins, Reubin R.   8151 Rugby Ave., Birmingham, AL

Mundy, Carl S.   Route 9, Box 315, Charlotte, NC

Murphy, George A., Jr.   120 North Drennar, Houston, TX

Nash, Gilbert D.   Onsted, MI

Noel, Lawrence M.   1710 Price Street, Lynchburg, VA

Nations, James W.   Box 12, Whittier, NC

Neaver, Walter   27 Main St., Torrington, CT

Nordman, Arthur E.   Box 86, Quinnesec, MI

Ofczarzak, Leo   Route #1, Box 255, Brenham, TX

Owens, Macey A.   113 Rhodes Ave., Lufkin, TX

Para, Robert F.   36 Pond St., Wester, MA

Pena, Dionisio F.   1501 17th Ave., Tampa, FL

Plante, John M.   139 Federal St., Bristol, CT

Plummer, Richard L.   2511 Vine Ave., Sioux City, IA

Prater, LeRoy C.   8 East Ashland St., Milford, IL

Prlain, Peter   717 ½ S. Main St., Butte, MT

Ravenelle, Rosario H.   65 River St., Southbridge, MA

Ray, Leonard C.   4516 Lafayette Ave., Fort Worth, TX

Reynolds, Claude A.   615 West 12th St., Beardstown, IL

Rhodea, Donald O.   2356 Evanston Ave., Muskegon, MI

Roberts, Orville J.   3599 Hillger, Detroit, MI

Robinson, Charles P.   c/o Mrs. G. G. Robinson, Box 482, Montpelier, ID

Robinson, Hurskin C.   Millport, AL

Rodriguez, Inocente   3 # M St., Smelter Town, TX

Rowlett, John   824 Southern Blvd., Bronx, NY

Scott, Wilbur   114 West Council St., Tomah, WI

Seifert, George B.   Route 2, Nazareth, PA

Sharon, Harold O.   1228 Benton Blvd., Kansas City, MO

Shaw, Herbert W.   35 Bay View Ave., Quincy, MA

Shields, Frank H.   P.O. Box 305, Mt. Vernon, IL

Simmons, Thomas R.   904 South 1st St., Temple, TX

Sims, Thomas H.   Avard, OK

Sinkovich, George E.   422 South Green St., Detroit, MI

Smith, James E.   Virginia, IL

Sneed, Fred M.   Route 2, Box 163, Murphy, NC

Stanley, Thomas A.   11421 Stewart Ave., Chicago, IL

Steffens, Roy E.   5707 Vanderbilt St., Dallas, TX

Stevenson, Stanley L.   Route #5, Buffalo Gap Rd., Abilene, TX

Stitt, Edward R.   1411 10th Ave., Scottsbluff, NE

Stokes, John A.   Dixon, MO

Stroebel, Donald F.   2804 South Wayne Ave., Fort Wayne, IN

Surine, Raymond L.   c/o Dorothy Eyestone, 212 West Madison, Lansing, MI

Sutley, Edward E.   RD #3, Bradford, PA

Tagliavia, Erasmo P.   38 Allen Pl., Fitchburg, MA

Talkington, Robert A.   Alvy, WV

"B" Company (continued)

Tallman, LeRoy   1209 North Raynor Ave., Joliet, IL

Tarulli, Michael A.   402 4th St., Brooklyn, NY

Terry, Harold H.   195 Chicago Ave., Marion, OH

Traum, Edgar   1913 Linden Ave., Baltimore, MD

Valenti, Gasper   691 Drew St., Brooklyn, NY

Veltre, Frank A.   Box 57, Alverda, PA

Villanueva, Israel V.   Box 179, Dilley, TX

Viveiros, Jose C.   72 Pleasant St., Seekonk, MA

Volek, Thomas A.   Box 22, Smock, PA

Waite, Raymond W.   R.D. #4, Wellington, OH

Watson, William J.   625 West 33rd St., Baltimore, MD

Weatherford, Ernest W.   1509 Filbert St., Flat B, Curtis Bay, Baltimore, MD

Weiler, William F.   1812 Charles St., Lafayette, IN

Wilkinson, Richard D.   1210 North Tejon, Colorado Springs, CO

Williams, Leo   1405 South Kansas, Wichita, KS

Wilson, Edward C.   Dandridge, TN

Wingfield, John R., Jr.   Goodwater, AL

Wood, William L.   803 Delmar St., Sikeston, MO

Wright, Oliver D.   Arab, AL

Yancy, Larry W.   Route #2, Arlington, KY

Young, Fred H.   8533 106th St., Richmond Hill, Long Island, NY

"C" Company

Adams, Charles E.   3413 Fenkell Ave., Detroit, MI

Arrowsmith, Franklin M.   804 W. 14th, Coffeyville, KS

Ayres, Zebina L.   Goddard, KS

Baird, Homer A.   Box #1, Pleasant Gap, PA

Baire, Joseph W.   436 Ketsham St., Indianapolis, IN

Barnes, Norman C.   47 Wake St., Napa, CA

Baron, Harry F.   1059 No. Ridgeway Ave., Chicago, IL

Boris, John A.   900 119th St., Chicago, IL

Boss, Andrew   7611 Normal Ave., Chicago, IL

Boxx, Leonard E.   R.F.D. #3, Box 308, Oceala, AR

Brewer, Burford L.   Route #1, Hamilton, MS

Brezgel, Aloysius S.   2501 S. 11th St., Milwaukee, WI

Brooks, Paul E.   606 S. Powell St., Bluefield, WV

Brown, Norbert J.   29929 Neles Rd., Hayward, CA

Buchanan, Joe B.   4216 Third St., Greenville, TX

Cantu, Abelardo H.   512 N. Cebolo St., San Antonio, TX

Carlson, Wilfred R.   1219 12th Ave., San Francisco, CA

Carter, Milton D.   Box 371, Rt. #9, Oklahoma City, OK

Castro, Raymond R.   Rt. #1, Box 95, Martinez, CA

Chavez, Fermin G.   Route 2, Box 549, Los Lunas, NM

Coakley, Raymond R.   R.F.D. #1; Bethany, WV

Cochran, William K.   1015 Duncan Ave., Duncan, OK

Colby, Ullyn S.   784 Buenta Vesta, Pomona, CA

Collins, James A.   Box 146, Ozark, MO

Conciardo, Samuel C.   248 West Ave., Buffalo, NY

Correia, Mariano   118 Sheldon St., Providence, RI

Crawford, Thurman R.   87 Wainwright Dr., Dayton, OH

Crotty, E. R., Jr.   510 ½ Second Ave., S. Charleston, WV

Curto, Danny R.   27 Le Roy Ave., Valhalla, NY

Cusimano, Peter J.   419 Foote Ave., Jamestown, NY

Davalos, Rudolfo G.   2015 Ft. Worth St., Bracketville, TX

Davis, Paul W.   R.F.D. #5, Midland, MI

De Chicko, Louis A.   8th & 24th, Beaver Falls, PA

Doss, Kenneth W.   Vivian, LA

Doughty, Stanley E.   Wells Rd., Cape Elizabeth, ME

Draper, Lee D.   4322 So. 21st, Omaha, NE

Du Marce, Harold W.   513 S. 6th St., Virginia, MN

Dyson, George R.   512 West Allen, Springfield, IL

Ehlert, Glenn H.   Dundee, IL

Evans, Lawrence F.   2419 West 67th St., Chicago, IL

Fernandez, Joseph L.   901 S. Main St., Victoria, TX

Ferris, Wendell O.   Route #6, Memphis, MO

Fogliani, Armando   356 N. Main St., Farmington, IL

Foley, Ernest J.   595 French St., Peshtigo, WI

Fones, Melvin M., Jr.   1007 Gibbon St., Alexandria, VA

Frolich, Vincent P.   27 Kempton St., Boston, MA

Gallo, Andy   1107 S. Mozart, Chicago, IL

Gibbens, Raymond W.   805 Chicago St., Dalhart, TX

Gonzales, Angel H.   91 Grace St., Perttleville, AZ

Graham, Albert D.   1006 9th Ave., Conway, SC

Griffin, Donald J.   San Luis Obispo, CA

Gustafson, Elmer J. H.   Rt. #2, Box 406, Austin, TX

"C" Company (continued)

Hamill, Curtis O. Rt. #2, Sturges, MS

Harris, Donald F. 822 29th St., Rock Island, IL

Harrison, Alred L. Baldwin, KS

Harrison, Clarence W. 11th St., Tell City, IN

Hartwick, Marvin D. England, AR

Hemphill, Jonny R. Hazelhurst, MS

Hiatt, Loyal G. 609 Molone St., Enid, OK

Higgins, Carl F. R.F.D. #2, Syracuse, NY

Hill, Oscar J. Groveland, FL

Hoegerl, John L. 1641 Fifth Ave., Pittsburgh, PA

Holdaway, Richard A. 209 1/2 West 6th St., The Dallas, OR

Howes, Charles J. Rockville, MD

Huffman, Max V. Box 596, Keefer, OK

Hughes, Warren W. R.F.D. #1, Edna, KS

Hulett, Dale E. 4249 S. Fox, Englewood, CO

Hulsey, Frank E. 810 Med Ave., Wewoka, OK

Hunt, John W. 142 Clark Place, Memphis, TN 4

Hunter, Frank J. 213 N. Arcadia, Colorado Spring, CO

Israel, Bernice R. Box 282, Thornton, CA

Ives, Donald V. R.F.D. #12, Box 414, Milwaukee, OR

Jackson, John B. R.F.D. #2, Bogalosa, LA

Jackson, Walter S. Kendalls Head, Eastport, ME

Jacobs, John W. 4317 Michigan, Covington, KY

Jimerson, Herman V. Gowanda, NY

Johnson, Eugene H. 108 West Acheson St., Denison, TX

Kelley, James L. 732 N. 7th St., Enid, OK

Kelley, W. T. Box 282, Melrose, NM

Kennedy, Norman W. 130 East Eldridge, Flint, MI

Kessell, William A. 3415 No. Kedzie Ave., Chicago, IL

Kniep, Erwin A. A. Byron, NE

Knudsen, Christian S. 528 Hilton Ave., Catonsville, MD

Komarynski, Jan Route #2, Hudson, MI

Konopka, Alexander J. 21 Ingraham St., Bristol, CT

Lehmann, Albert J., Jr. Maple Ave., Selkirk, NY

Lobach, Harry S. 500 Ave. A, Bismark, ND

Lordi, John J. 100 S. St., Newark, NJ

Lowery, Jay L. 1332 Shirley Ave., El Monte, CA

Martinez, David Box 505, Carlsbad, CA

"C" Company (continued)

McAffee, Max C. 203 Loma Vista, El Segundo, CA

McCrary, Herbert W. 821 6th Ave., Texas City, TX

Mihaly, Paul, Jr. Route #2, Gansevoort, NY

Miller, Donald H. Sullivan, IL

Miller, Frank E. Box 482, Williamsburg, VA

Murray, William F. 8300 Cooper Ave., Glendales, Long Island, NY

Natzke, Emil A. 2636 Crane Ave., Detroit, MI

Nick, Sam Marksville, LA

Nissen, Arnold P. Route #4, Exira, IA

Norgan, Arthur W. State Park Dr., Bay City, MI

North, Glenn L. 116 ½ N. 9th St., Dekalb, IL

Papace, Vincent J. 315 Prospect Ave., Brooklyn, NY

Pardy, Harold 1312 East Myers, Hazel Park, MI

Parnell, Joseph Stephenville, TX

Pastiro, Joe 525 Fanning St., Shreveport, LA

Perotka, Edward J. 1855 Edw. Rd., Madison, IL

Perry, Leon G. Route #2, Box 168, Edmond, OK

Pollard, James C. Route #1, Warsaw, MO

Pomeroy, Wray S. 626 Zeyne St., Anaheim, CA

Rapson, George A. Harbor Beach, MI

Rave, Richard A. R.F.D. #13, Box 539, Tacoma, WA

Rice, David A. 210 Bank St., Lodi, OH

Roach, Rufus H. R.F.D. #1, Milford, DE

Roberts, Hubert L. Route #1, West Terra Haute, IN

Rose, Charles L. 111 Sante Fe St., Alva, OK

Sacksteder, Raymond A. Alexandria Pike, Cold Spring, KY

Scala, Pasquale C. 1030 West Taylor St., Chicago, IL

Selby, Roger N. 11 Fayetteville St., Van Buren, AR

Simmons, Louis G. Box 76, Ceresco, MI

Sinclair, Donald J. 1433 Hewett Ave., St. Paul, MN

Sleasman, Jack B. Pacific Beach, WA

Smith, James E., Jr. Route #2, Bullard, TX

Snyder, William H. 1862 Major St., Bethlehem, PA

Spaulding, Victor I. 4601 Harrison St., Sioux City, IA

Stephens, Martin J. St. Francisville, IL

Stouffer, James F. Star Route, Scottsdale, PA

Stroud, Lee E. Box 193, Chelsea, OK

Stroup, Harold W. 210 Bowman St., Mansfield, OH

Sturgill, Kenneth Dorchester, VA

"C" Company (continued)

Tate, Joseph H.   Malden, MO

Teas, Edward J.   Teas Nursery Co., Houston 6, TX

Thomas, Wylie W.   610 Ave. O, Lubbock, TX

Thompson, Elbert G.   Portland, MO

Tomlinson, George   North Berger, NJ

Topham, Thomas W.   23 Montgomery Ave., Upper Darby, PA

Trella, Angelo   12755 Horn Ave., Blue Island, IL

Uliasz, Bernard J.   3139 Washington Blvd., Chicago, IL

Urban, Frank V.   Chetapo, KS

Vasily, George M.   1062 Lara St., Los Angeles, CA

Vega, Fidencio P.   611 N. Capia St., El Paso, TX

Vilmain, George T.   Eagle Grove, IA

Vyvjala, Alfred   Smithville, TX

Wagner, Julius E.   P.O. Box 2564, Houston 1, TX

Weisel, Duane B.   5123 West 21st, Los Angeles, CA

Williams, John H.   1314 Chew St., Allentown, PA

Williams, Paul   Stigler, OK

Wilson, Reginald E.   614 East 8th St., San Angelo, TX

Winn, William F.   3136 S. 2nd Wist, Salt Lake City, UT

Wisnieski, Stanley   1731 West 4th St., Dunellen, NJ

Wittner, Charles J.   909 Williams St., River Forest, IL

Wood, Russell J.   R.F.D. #2, Box 462, Roanoke, VA

Wright, Raymond E.   121 Douglas Ave., Dixon, IL

Zebell, Calvin E.   8156 Vincennes Ave., Chicago, IL

Medical Detachment

Allred, Russell D.   RR #5, Norman, OK

Bartosevich, Paul P.   11 Main St., Upper Lehigh, PA

Boudreau, William F.   180 Cedar St., Somerville, MA

Burton, Carl W.   511 West Jenny, Bay City, MI

Fry, Donald A.   10448 Eastbourne Ave., Los Angeles 24, CA

Gnade, Eugene   Old Monroe, MO

Hornberger, Ray L.   345 Russell Ave., Williamsport, PA

Iannelli, John   22 Falcon St., East Boston, MA

Lentz, Paul C.   RR #1, Oshkosh, WI

Saville, Donald K.   258 Osmun, Pontiac, MI

Scott, Russell L.   Chesterfield, IL

Seabrook, William   510 Wood St., Fiqua, OH

Spencer, Gerald F.   4257 Northeast Halsey, Portland 13, OR

Army of the United States

CERTIFICATE OF SERVICE

This is to certify that

WILLIAM C KING   O 511 656   Captain

45th Engineer General Service Regiment

honorably served in active Federal Service

in the Army of the United States from

31 March 1943   *to*   25 May 1946

Given at   SEPARATION CENTER, Camp Atterbury, Indiana

on the   25 th   *day of*   May   *19* 46

E. A. SCHLENDER,
MAJOR, CE.

MILITARY RECORD AND REPORT OF SEPARATION
CERTIFICATE OF SERVICE

1. LAST NAME - FIRST NAME - MIDDLE INITIAL	2. ARMY SERIAL NUMBER	3. AUS. GRADE	4. ARM OR SERVICE	5. COMPONENT
KING WILLIAM C	O 511 656	Capt	CE	ORC

6. ORGANIZATION	7. DATE OF RELIEF FROM ACTIVE DUTY	8. PLACE OF SEPARATION
45th Engineer General Service Regiment	25 May 46	Separation Center Camp Atterbury Ind

9. PERMANENT ADDRESS FOR MAILING PURPOSES	10. DATE OF BIRTH	11. PLACE OF BIRTH
208 Gladstone Rd Pittsburgh 17 Pa	11 Aug 21	Pittsburgh Pa

12. ADDRESS FROM WHICH EMPLOYMENT WILL BE SOUGHT	13. COLOR EYES	14. COLOR HAIR	15. HEIGHT	16. WEIGHT	17. NO. OF DEPENDENTS
Will Resume Education	Blue	Brown	6'1"	150 LBS.	0

18. RACE			19. MARITAL STATUS			20. U.S. CITIZEN		21. CIVILIAN OCCUPATION AND NO.
WHITE	NEGRO	OTHER (specify)	SINGLE	MARRIED	OTHER (specify)	YES	NO	
X			X			X		Student X-02

MILITARY HISTORY

SELECTIVE SERVICE DATA ▶

22. REGISTERED		23. LOCAL S.S. BOARD NUMBER	24. COUNTY AND STATE	25. HOME ADDRESS AT TIME OF ENTRY ON ACTIVE DUTY
YES	NO			
	X		None	See #9

26. DATE OF ENTRY ON ACTIVE DUTY	27. MILITARY OCCUPATIONAL SPECIALTY AND NO.
31 Mar 43	Platoon Leader 1337 Operations and Training Staff Officer 2162 Supply and Evacuation Officer 4470

28. BATTLES AND CAMPAIGNS

India-Burma GO105 WD45   Central Burma GO105 WD45

29. DECORATIONS AND CITATIONS

American Theater Service Medal   Asiatic Pacific Service Medal   Victory Medal

30. WOUNDS RECEIVED IN ACTION

None

31. SERVICE SCHOOLS ATTENDED Camouflage School Officers Candidate School (CE) Engineer Construction and Tactics	32. SERVICE OUTSIDE CONTINENTAL U. S. AND RETURN		
	DATE OF DEPARTURE	DESTINATION	DATE OF ARRIVAL
	14 Dec 43	Asiatic Pacific	13 Feb 44
33. REASON AND AUTHORITY FOR SEPARATION Reld fr AD RR1-1 (D) MO Hq Repl Depot #3 8 Feb 46 1st Ind Hq Cp Stoneman Calif 8 Mar 46	11 Feb 46	U S	8 Mar 46

34.	CURRENT TOUR OF ACTIVE DUTY					35.	EDUCATION (years)		
CONTINENTAL SERVICE			FOREIGN SERVICE				GRAMMAR SCHOOL	HIGH SCHOOL	COLLEGE
YEARS	MONTHS	DAYS	YEARS	MONTHS	DAYS		8	4	4
0	11	0	2	2	25				

INSURANCE NOTICE

IMPORTANT IF PREMIUM IS NOT PAID WHEN DUE OR WITHIN THIRTY-ONE DAYS THEREAFTER, INSURANCE WILL LAPSE. MAKE CHECKS OR MONEY ORDERS PAYABLE TO THE TREASURER OF THE U. S. AND FORWARD TO COLLECTIONS SUBDIVISION, VETERANS ADMINISTRATION, WASHINGTON 25, D. C.

36. KIND OF INSURANCE			37. HOW PAID		38. Effective Date of Allotment Discontinuance	39. Date of Next Premium Due (one month after 38)	40. PREMIUM DUE EACH MONTH	41. INTENTION OF VETERAN TO		
Nat. Serv.	U.S. Govt.	None	Allotment	Direct to V.A.				Continue	Continue only	Discontinue
X				X			$ 6.60		$	X

	43. REMARKS (This space for completion of above items or entry of other items specified in W. D. Directives)
RIGHT THUMB PRINT	On Terminal Leave from 16 Mar 46 to 25 May 46 Inclusive Lapel Button Issued ASR Score (2 Sep 45) -63

44. SIGNATURE OF OFFICER BEING SEPARATED	45. PERSONNEL OFFICER (Type name, grade and organization - signature)
William C. King	H V MILLER 2nd Lt MAC *H V Miller*

WD AGO FORM 53 - 98
November 1944

This form supersedes all previous editions of WD AGO Forms 53 and 280 for officers entitled to a Certificate of Service, which will not be used after receipt of this revision.